# Depressive Disorders

**Diseases and Disorders**

ReferencePoint Press®

San Diego, CA

## Other books in the Compact Research Diseases and Disorders set:

*For a complete list of titles please visit www.referencepointpress.com.

COMPACT *Research*

# Depressive Disorders

### Carla Mooney

**Diseases and Disorders**

ReferencePoint
Press®

San Diego, CA

Picture credits:
Cover: Dreamstime and iStockphoto.com
Maury Aaseng: 33–34, 46–47, 59–61, 74–76
Thinkstock Images: 12, 17

LIBRARY OF CONGRESS CATALOGING-IN-PUBLICATION DATA

Mooney, Carla, 1970–
   Depressive disorders / by Carla Mooney.
     pages ; cm. -- (Compact research series)
   Audience: Grade 9 to 12.
   Includes bibliographical references and index.
   ISBN 978-1-60152-504-8 (hardback) -- ISBN 1-60152-504-4 (hardback)
 1. Depression, Mental--Popular works. I. Title.
   RC537.M6644   2013
   362.2'5--dc23

                                            2012036681

# Contents

# Foreword

**"Where is the knowledge we have lost in information?"**

—T.S. Eliot, "The Rock."

A s modern civilization continues to evolve, its ability to create, store, distribute, and access information expands exponentially. The explosion of information from all media continues to increase at a phenomenal rate. By 2020 some experts predict the worldwide information base will double every seventy-three days. While access to diverse sources of information and perspectives is paramount to any democratic society, information alone cannot help people gain knowledge and understanding. Information must be organized and presented clearly and succinctly in order to be understood. The challenge in the digital age becomes not the creation of information, but how best to sort, organize, enhance, and present information.

ReferencePoint Press developed the *Compact Research* series with this challenge of the information age in mind. More than any other subject area today, researching current issues can yield vast, diverse, and unqualified information that can be intimidating and overwhelming for even the most advanced and motivated researcher. The *Compact Research* series offers a compact, relevant, intelligent, and conveniently organized collection of information covering a variety of current topics ranging from illegal immigration and deforestation to diseases such as anorexia and meningitis.

The series focuses on three types of information: objective single-author narratives, opinion-based primary source quotations, and facts and statistics. The clearly written objective narratives provide context and reliable background information. Primary source quotes are carefully selected and cited, exposing the reader to differing points of view, and facts and statistics sections aid the reader in evaluating perspectives. Presenting these key types of information creates a richer, more balanced learning experience.

For better understanding and convenience, the series enhances information by organizing it into narrower topics and adding design features that make it easy for a reader to identify desired content. For example, in *Compact Research: Illegal Immigration*, a chapter covering the economic impact of illegal immigration has an objective narrative explaining the various ways the economy is impacted, a balanced section of numerous primary source quotes on the topic, followed by facts and full-color illustrations to encourage evaluation of contrasting perspectives.

The ancient Roman philosopher Lucius Annaeus Seneca wrote, "It is quality rather than quantity that matters." More than just a collection of content, the *Compact Research* series is simply committed to creating, finding, organizing, and presenting the most relevant and appropriate amount of information on a current topic in a user-friendly style that invites, intrigues, and fosters understanding.

# Depressive Disorders at a Glance

## Depressive Disorders Defined

A depressive disorder is a mental illness that involves a debilitating sadness, with symptoms that affect a person's body, mood, and thoughts. Depressive disorders interfere with patients' ability to participate in daily life and to take care of themselves properly, both physically and mentally.

## Many Forms of Depression

There are several different forms of depressive disorders. These include major depression, dysthymia, and postpartum depression. Symptoms may vary, depending on the disorder.

## Prevalence of Depression

According to the Centers for Disease Control and Prevention, approximately 10 percent of people in the United States over the age of eighteen suffer from a depressive disorder.

## Signs and Symptoms

Symptoms of a depressive disorder include an unending sadness, changes in sleep patterns and appetite, fatigue, and feelings of worthlessness and hopelessness.

# Causes

Most experts believe that depressive disorders are caused by a combination of genetic, biological, and environmental factors.

# Effects of Depression

Depressive disorders often impair a person's ability to sleep, eat, and work and damage relationships with family and friends. Depressive disorders can also cause people to feel bad about themselves, leading to unhealthy behaviors such as eating disorders, substance abuse, and self-injury.

# Treatment

Most people treated for depression see an improvement in their symptoms within four to six weeks. Medication, talk therapy, electroconvulsive therapy, and lifestyle changes have all been effective treatments for depression.

# Prognosis

Depression is often a long-term, or chronic, condition. Effective treatments can manage symptoms so that people with depression can lead productive lives.

# Overview

Sadness touches everybody at some point during his or her life. It is normal to feel sad and cry when a loved one dies, after experiencing a trauma, or after being rejected by peers. For most people, feelings of sadness pass within a couple of days or so. For others, a persistent, debilitating sadness lingers and becomes more serious. Other symptoms emerge, such as insomnia, loss of appetite, lack of concentration, and irritability. Depression and its symptoms interfere with a person's ability to function in daily life and affect his or her thoughts, moods, and actions. Depressive disorders include major depression, dysthymia, seasonal affective disorder, postpartum depression, and bipolar disorder. The number, longevity, and severity of symptoms for each depressive disorder may vary. In order to feel better, many people need treatment to ease their symptoms. Without treatment, depressive symptoms may last for weeks, months, or even years.

According to the Centers for Disease Control and Prevention, approximately 10 percent of people in the United States over the age of eighteen suffer from a depressive disorder. Major depression is the most common depressive disorder, with about one in fifteen American adults affected by it. In a given year, approximately 1.5 percent of American adults over age eighteen are affected by a milder depressive disorder called dysthymia. Bipolar disorder, a depressive disorder that causes alternating periods of depression (lows) and mania (highs), affects about 2.6 percent of American adults.

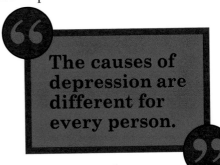

**The causes of depression are different for every person.**

In the United States, women are twice as likely as men to be diagnosed and treated for major depression. As children, boys and girls have equal rates of depression. When girls reach adolescence, however, they are more likely to become depressed. As girls mature into women, they continue to have an increased risk of depression.

If a person has had depression in the past, his or her chances of developing it again increase. Approximately 50 percent of people who have experienced a depressive episode will have future episodes. People who have experienced one type of depressive disorder are also more likely to experience another type as well. For example, more than half of those suffering from dysthymia will eventually develop major depression, say researchers from Harvard Medical School. Because they are likely to recur, most depressive disorders are considered long-term, or chronic, illnesses.

## A Variety of Symptoms

Depression symptoms can vary greatly. Feelings of sadness over a loss or a traumatic event are a normal part of life. But when those feelings persist, and when they are combined with several other symptoms, this might be a sign of a depressive disorder. People with depressive disorders generally experience a severe sadness that interferes with their lives. They may lose interest in activities they once enjoyed and withdraw from family and friends. Feelings of hopelessness and worthlessness are also common. Depressive disorders cause physical symptoms like headaches, stomachaches, and fatigue. Sleeping and eating patterns may also change.

Lindsay Wright is a professional golfer on the LPGA tour, who has

*Depressive disorders go beyond feelings of sadness that everyone experiences at one time or another. Clinical depression is marked by persistent, debilitating sadness that leads to insomnia, loss of appetite, lack of concentration, and irritability.*

struggled with depression. "People think, 'Depression—oh, just get over it if you're in a bad mood,' or whatever," says Wright. "It really impacts you physically, and . . . when you're not sleeping and you can't concentrate or focus and the other symptoms with it, it just gets you down, and it's a bit of a nightmare." At first Wright tried to tough it out and play through her symptoms, as she had been taught to do as an athlete. "Where I played golf and grew up, it's like, you just get on with it and do it, get over it and move on," she says. Eventually, Wright realized that she could not manage her depression alone. While watching television one day, she listened to a woman talk about depression and recognized herself in the woman's story. Soon afterward, Wright sought help. "When I did go to the doctor and got a diagnosis, I realized, 'Jeez, I really do have a problem here,'" Wright says.[1]

## What Causes Depressive Disorders?

The causes of depressive disorders are not well understood. Mental health experts believe that depression has no single cause. Instead, they suspect that a complex combination of biological, environmental, and genetic factors interact in people who become depressed.

The causes of depression are different for every person. Two people may have similar depressive symptoms, but the causes behind their symptoms may be entirely different. Some people may become depressed due to changes in brain chemicals, while others find their depression is triggered by a significant, traumatic event in their lives. Depression can also be triggered by medications or other illnesses. Each person reacts differently to these factors, making it difficult to predict who will develop depression.

Mental health experts believe that chemical imbalances in the brain are one factor in depression. Chemicals called neurotransmitters carry messages from the brain to different parts of the body. In people with depression, levels of these chemicals can be too high or too low and the messages can be lost or distorted, leading to depressive symptoms. Researchers say that many chemicals are involved in how the brain regulates mood, which adds to the complexity of establishing the cause of depression. "It is not a simple matter of one chemical being too low and another too high. Rather many chemicals are involved, working both inside and outside nerve cells. There are millions, even billions, of chemical reactions that make up the dynamic system that is responsible for your mood, your perceptions, and the way you experience life," say researchers from Harvard Medical School.[2]

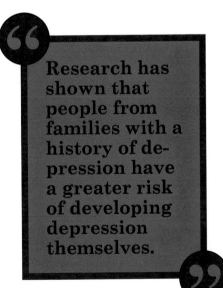

Research has shown that people from families with a history of depression have a greater risk of developing depression themselves.

Hormone imbalances may be another factor in depression. Researchers know that some hormones directly affect the brain chemistry that controls emotions and mood. They have found that many people with depression have abnormal levels of certain hormones in their blood. For example, cortisol is a hormone that helps the body regulate its reaction to stress. About 50 percent of people with clinical depression have an excess of cortisol in their blood. Researchers are also investigating the link between hormones and depression in women. Because adult women are twice as likely as men to develop depression, mental health experts believe that female hormones may play a role in depression. To learn more, they are focusing studies on women at certain points in their lives when hormone levels change, during puberty, menstruation, pregnancy, and menopause.

Environmental factors can also increase a person's risk of developing depression. For many people, a stressful event such as the death of a loved one, job loss, or end of a relationship causes normal sadness. For some people, however, these events can trigger a severe depressive episode. Other environmental factors that can influence depression include traumatic events, injury, and abuse. How a person handles stress and other life events and the availability of a support network may influence whether that person develops depression. Yet environmental factors do not affect all people in the same way. Mental health experts believe that environmental factors can trigger depression in people who are already genetically susceptible to the illness.

## Inheriting Depression

No one is immune to depression; it affects people of all ages and from all backgrounds. Nonetheless, certain groups of people tend to develop depression more often than others do. Research has shown that people from families with a history of depression have a greater risk of developing depression themselves. Persons with a parent or sibling suffering from major depression are one-and-a-half to three times more likely to develop it themselves.

Although research suggests a genetic link to depression, scientists are still learning which genes are involved and how they influence who develops it. "We are just beginning to make our way through the maze of influences on depression, and this is an important step toward understanding what may be happening at the genetic and molecular levels,"[3] says Michele Pergadia, a researcher from Washington University in St. Louis who is studying genes and depression.

# How Do Depressive Disorders Affect People?

Depression can affect a person's life in many ways. It can affect how a person performs at work or at school. The person may have difficulty concentrating or may miss days because of the illness. According to the National Institute of Mental Health (NIMH), major depression is the leading cause of disability in the United States for people aged fifteen to forty-four. It costs US businesses billions of dollars each year in medical expenses, worker absences, and lost productivity.

A woman named Tanya says that depression had a severe impact on her life and relationships. "I was so clinically depressed it was impossible to even get out of bed. I felt spiritually, mentally and physically paralyzed. . . . I was self destructive. I drank alcohol, took pills and was horribly angry. I was in a negative and unhealthy space and had no idea what to do,"[4] she says.

People with depression may act differently around family and friends. They may withdraw and spend more time alone. Favorite activities may no longer interest them. Minor events may trigger crying, anger, or fights. Because their behavior appears erratic, family and friends may have a difficult time understanding why they are acting differently. This may strain or damage relationships. Forty-two-year-old Stacy from Calgary, Alberta, Canada, found herself easily tired and unable to concentrate or cope with pressure when dealing with depression. She cried frequently. Afraid that people would react negatively if she talked about her depression, Stacy says that she began to draw away from friends and family. "A good friend at work talked to me once after I told her what was going on, and then I never heard from her again," says Stacy. "I pretty much shut everyone out, because I was afraid of what others would say or think."[5]

Depression also has a noticeable emotional impact on those who suffer from it. Some people experience extreme emotions for no apparent reason; others lack confidence and suffer from low self-esteem, which adds to their own negative feelings about themselves. Kevin Solomons, a clinical associate professor of psychiatry at the University of British Columbia in Vancouver, Canada, says that low self-esteem is a key component of depression. "If you think of yourself as worthless and hopeless, the emotion that corresponds is unhappiness and misery,"[6] says Solomons.

## Risky Behavior

People who are depressed are more likely to abuse alcohol, drugs, or cigarettes than people who are not. They use substances to help them cope with overwhelming feelings of sadness. According to the US Department of Health and Human Services, more than 21 percent of adults who had experienced a depressive episode within the previous year had abused alcohol or drugs, as compared with 8 percent of adults who had abused these substances but did not have depression.

Using drugs and alcohol to numb feelings may work in the short term, but substance abuse makes a person feel worse over time. "In trying to self-medicate with alcohol, people don't realize they're using a depressant," says David MacIsaac, a psychologist licensed in New York and New Jersey and a faculty member of the New York Institute for Psychoanalytic Self Psychology. "In point of fact, it will intensify their depression."[7] Teenager Pete began using drugs and alcohol at age fifteen to deal with his depression. "Through my drinking, I went through bouts of depression day in [and] day out, usually crying myself sick to get to sleep. I lost all train of thought and my life ceased to become anything but drink and drugs,"[8] he says. Depression has also been connected to other risky behaviors, such as cutting and other self-injury, unprotected and promiscuous sex, and eating disorders.

> "People who are depressed are more likely to abuse alcohol, drugs, or cigarettes than people who are not."

## Suicide

According to the Centers for Disease Control and Prevention, more than thirty-three thousand people in the United States kill themselves each year. Of those, more than 90 percent have a mental disorder, most commonly a depressive or substance abuse disorder. In addition, Harvard Medical School reports that for every completed suicide, there are another estimated eleven suicide attempts. For teens and young adults, depression is the number one risk factor for suicide.

*People who are depressed often turn to alcohol, drugs, or cigarettes in hopes of finding relief from lingering and overwhelming feelings of sadness and hopelessness.*

What triggers a depressed person to take his or her own life varies from person to person. Many times, the anger, despair, and hopelessness that accompany depression lead a person to think that death is the only escape. Nineteen-year-old Ashley says that depression led to her suicide attempt. Although she was a popular, straight-A student, Ashley struggled with feelings of unhappiness. When she left home for boarding school in the ninth grade, her unhappiness worsened. Ashley began thinking about hurting herself, had panic attacks, and found it difficult to concentrate. "I just wasn't myself. I didn't want to live and felt worthless,"[9] she says. After seeing her family doctor, Ashley began taking antianxiety and antidepressant medication. Eventually, Ashley began planning her suicide. One night, when she felt herself at a breaking point, Ashley overdosed on her medication. She woke up her father, who rushed her to the emergency room, where she was treated.

## Diagnosing Depression

When multiple depressive symptoms persist, mental health experts recommend that a person seek professional help. Untreated depression can linger for weeks, months, or years. As time passes, it often grows worse and become more difficult to treat. Untreated depression also increases a person's risk for future episodes of depression.

A doctor or mental health expert can diagnose patients with a depressive disorder. To diagnose depression, the mental health professional will ask patients about their feelings, experiences, and physical symptoms. During the evaluation, the mental health professional will also look for any medications, illnesses, or physical conditions that may be causing depressive symptoms. Some types of strokes, thyroid disorders, and contraceptives can cause the same symptoms as a depressive disorder. If a depressive disorder is diagnosed, patients will work with their doctor or therapist to develop an appropriate treatment plan.

Researchers are also hopeful that depression may one day be diagnosed with a simple blood test. In a 2012 study, scientists at Northwestern University School of Medicine in Chicago were able to identify genetic markers with an experimental blood test. The scientists found eleven genetic markers in the blood of adolescents with untreated major depression that nondepressed teens did not have. "These 11 genes are probably the tip of the iceberg because depression is a complex illness.

But it's an entree into a much bigger phenomenon that has to be explored. It clearly indicates we can diagnose from blood and create a blood diagnosis test for depression,"[10] says study author Eva Redei, a professor of psychiatry and behavioral sciences at Northwestern University's Feinberg School of Medicine.

## What Treatments Are Available for Depressive Disorders?

Although depression is a serious illness, it can be treated. Most people learn to manage depression with treatment and so lead a productive life. According to the National Institute of Mental Health, up to 80 percent of people treated for depression show improvement within four to six weeks.

Most depression treatments involve some type of psychotherapy, also known as talk therapy. Talk therapy can take place in individual, group, or family sessions. During a therapy session, a person talks with a mental health expert about the person's feelings and problems. Talking about these issues can help the person learn to recognize unhealthy thoughts and behaviors and use strategies to replace them with productive ones. One of the most common types of talk therapy is cognitive behavioral therapy (CBT), in which the patient learns techniques to change negative thoughts and behaviors into more positive ones.

Research has shown that while mild depression can be treated by talk therapy alone, more severe cases are most effectively treated with a combination of therapy and medication. Antidepressant medications are widely used to treat depression. These medications affect how brain chemicals called neurotransmitters function and control mood. Several types of antidepressant medications treat depressive disorders, including selective serotonin reuptake inhibitors (SSRIs), tricyclics, and monoamine oxidase inhibitors (MAOIs). Experts estimate that 50 percent of unsuccessfully treated cases of depression result from people not taking their medica-

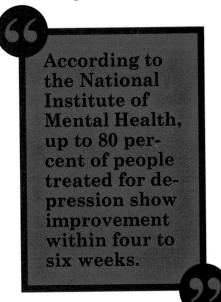

According to the National Institute of Mental Health, up to 80 percent of people treated for depression show improvement within four to six weeks.

tions properly. Unpleasant side effects, financial costs, and short-term improvement of symptoms all can cause people to stop taking their antidepressant medication.

In some cases, traditional talk therapy and medication is not enough to relieve depressive symptoms. When this occurs, other treatments, such as hospitalization, electroconvulsive therapy (ECT), or nerve stimulation therapy may be considered. Up to 10 percent of major depressive episodes require hospitalization. This occurs most often when a person is suicidal or exhibits life-threatening behavior. For those who are severely depressed, suicidal, or experiencing severe mania, doctors may consider electroconvulsive therapy, in which short electrical pulses trigger a seizure in the brain. Recent advances in nerve stimulation therapies such as transcranial magnetic stimulation (TMS) and vagus nerve stimulation (VNS) have shown success in relieving symptoms for patients with treatment-resistant depression.

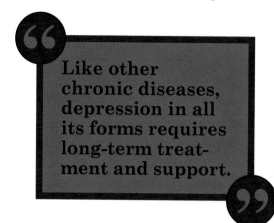

Like other chronic diseases, depression in all its forms requires long-term treatment and support.

## Lifestyle Changes

For many people with depression, making simple lifestyle changes has improved their symptoms and made it easier to live with their illness. These changes include getting exercise, reducing stress, getting enough sleep, and eating right. Other people use activities like writing in journals or creating art or music as healthy ways to express their emotions. "Journaling was one of those coping skills and it became my lifeline. I would journal my thoughts and feelings every day,"[11] says Tanya.

Many people with depression have a solid support system to help them successfully manage their illness. Some turn to family members, friends, or peer groups for support. Stacy from Calgary says that depression support groups help her feel not so alone. She has organized a peer support group at her local church, where members share stories about depression and coping techniques. "Speaking openly about depression to people who are experiencing it helps you know you're not alone,"[12] she says.

## Not a Choice

For years, depression had been misunderstood. Everyone was expected to deal with the normal setbacks of life, and those setbacks include feeling sad. People could not distinguish between such normal periods of sadness and the persistent lethargy of depression. "You see people every day thinking you should just 'suck it up,'"[13] says Stacy. Today, experts know that depression is a mental illness, not a choice. Like other chronic diseases, depression in all its forms requires long-term treatment and support. Although finding the right treatment may take time, it can happen eventually.

With effective treatment, support, and lifestyle adjustments, many people with depression can learn to live happy, healthy, and productive lives. "The concept of recovery needs reintroduction," says Patrick Corrigan, director of the National Consortium on Stigma and Empowerment at the Illinois Institute of Technology in Chicago, about depression. "People need hope, and the fact is that most people do recover."[14]

# What Are Depressive Disorders?

**❝I finally realized that if I didn't accept that depression was a disease, I couldn't begin to get through it. I have to tell myself every day, 'You have a disease, lighten up on yourself.'❞**

—Chuck Bennett (pseudonym), a Chicago businessman who was diagnosed with depression in his twenties.

**❝Depression was no longer just part of me—it was all of me.❞**

—Jenny Stamos, a patient with dysthymia.

**D**epression is not simply a passing blue mood; it is a persistent feeling of sadness that interferes with daily life, making it difficult to perform regular daily tasks or to take proper care of oneself. Along with sadness, common symptoms include decreased interest in activities, loss of self-confidence, and a sense of worthlessness. The presence of these symptoms—how strong they are and how long they last—helps distinguish depression from normal sadness. Without treatment, depression can last for weeks, months, or even years.

Depression affects a person's body, mood, and thoughts. It interferes with daily life and functioning, affecting sleep, appetite, energy levels, and relationships with others. Many people with depression find that they have difficulty performing simple tasks or even taking proper care of themselves. They might not have the energy to participate in their usual activities. They might even neglect personal hygiene. Family and friends often feel frustrated and angry when dealing with a person with depression. They may wonder why the person cannot just get over their sadness. The fact is few people recover from clinical depression without some sort of long-term help.

Depressive disorders come in several forms. Each form of depression may vary in the number of symptoms, as well as their severity and longevity. Some of the most common depressive disorders are major depression, dysthymia, seasonal affective disorder, postpartum depression, and bipolar disorder.

## Major Depression

One of the most common forms of depression is major depression, also known as clinical depression or unipolar depression. Often disabling, major depression can prevent one from fulfilling the tasks of normal daily life. Common symptoms include overwhelming sadness, decreased interest in activities, difficulty concentrating, loss of self-confidence, and a sense of worthlessness. Most people with major depression need treatment in order to feel better. Jennisse Peatick, a thirty-six-year-old from Hillsborough, New Jersey, says that depression feels like a heaviness that makes it hard to get out of bed. "I am in the bottom of a well and it is a very gray cloudy day and I am looking up at this insurmountable cloudy day and I can't climb out," she says. "It is silent and very isolating."[15]

> One of the most common forms of depression is major depression, also known as clinical depression or unipolar depression.

Depression can also affect a person's sleep habits, appetite, and energy levels. Some people may experience physical and mental symptoms such as fatigue, headaches, stomachaches, and suicidal thoughts. Each person may experience different symptoms. Some may become lethargic, while others feel agitated. Some people with depression may not be able to sleep, while others feel tired all the time. "My depression intertwines with anxiety. Together they have caused me migraines, stomachaches, painful joints, and an all-over heaviness that makes me loath to do anything. Most recently, I have had a terrible time sleeping,"[16] says Sue Fagalde Lick, a depression patient.

Major depression is most commonly diagnosed in people aged twenty-five to forty-four, yet it can strike at any age. Women are twice as likely as men to develop major depression. Major depression also runs in families. If a parent or sibling has the disorder, a person's risk of developing depression increases by one-and-a-half to three times.

> "Although the specific causes of SAD are unknown, most experts agree that too little exposure to light plays a role in triggering the disorder.

If untreated, major depression can last for years. A single episode may last from two weeks up to several months. Some people may experience only a single episode during their lives. For others, depression is a chronic illness, causing them to experience multiple episodes of depression separated by periods of normal moods.

Major depression may be related to certain medical illnesses. According to the Depression and Bipolar Support Alliance, up to one-fourth of patients with cancer, stroke, or diabetes develop depression. In addition, 50 to 75 percent of patients with anorexia or bulimia also experience depression. These people are dealing with the stress of their medical illnesses, which may cause them to become less independent or require lifestyle changes. These challenges can make the person more likely to develop depression. In addition, a person with major depression is more likely to have other health conditions such as alcohol and drug abuse, anxiety and panic disorders, and obsessive-compulsive disorders.

## Dysthymia

Dysthymia or dysthymic disorder is a milder but longer-lasting form of depression. People with dysthymia may experience changes in appetite, sleeping habits, and energy levels. They may have a hard time concentrating or making decisions. The symptoms may not be severe enough to disable a person, but they can disrupt normal functioning or cause the person to feel ill. To be diagnosed with dysthymia, a patient must experience a continuously depressed mood for at least two years. Women are two to three times more likely than men to be diagnosed with dysthymia. According to Harvard Medical School, approximately 6 percent of the US population has had an episode of dysthymia at some point in their lives.

Because dysthymia's symptoms are mild and often begin at an early age, many people do not realize that that the persistent sadness they experience is abnormal. For this reason, people with dysthymia often wait years before seeking treatment. Delayed treatment can result in a worsening of symptoms or the appearance of new ones. Early treatment, on the other hand, can help patients avoid more serious depressive or mental health disorders and other problems, such as substance abuse or difficulties in school or at work.

Having dysthymia makes a person more likely to develop major depression. According to Harvard Medical School, more than half of patients with dysthymia will eventually have an episode of major depression. In some cases, a patient will develop both disorders at the same time. This condition is called double depression. People with double depression have a greater risk for repeated major depressive episodes. They may also have more difficulty recovering from depression.

## Seasonal Affective Disorder

When depression occurs in a seasonal pattern, a person may have seasonal affective disorder (SAD). SAD affects a person at specific times or seasons during the year. Although the specific causes of SAD are unknown, most experts agree that too little exposure to light plays a role in triggering the disorder. "Light does more than just enable us to see," says Dr. Norman Rosenthal, author of *Winter Blues*. He says that light has an effect on hormones such as serotonin and melatonin, which are involved in regulating mood, energy, and appetite. "The hormone melatonin, which is secreted at night, can be suppressed by light," Dr. Rosenthal says. "Studies have also shown that light influences serotonin . . . pathways in the brain, the same neurotransmitter systems known to be affected in people with general depression."[17] Women are more likely than men to be affected by SAD. Those who live in higher latitudes, where there are more hours of winter darkness, have a higher risk for SAD as well.

According to Michael Young, an associate professor in the Institute of Psychology at the Illinois Institute of Technology, a person with SAD may feel normal and happy in the spring and summer but every winter will fall back into a depressive state. During this time, the patient may feel sluggish and have little energy. He or she might sleep or eat more than usual, craving carbohydrates that temporarily boost low levels of serotonin. "I've always seen a drastic change in my personality from spring and summer to fall and winter, and it got worse as I got older,"[18] says Rick Bach, fifty-four, a painter from West Hartford, Connecticut. A less common form of SAD involves depressive symptoms during the summer months.

## Postpartum Depression

Many women experience the "baby blues," a short period of sadness that occurs three to seven days after the birth of a child. For some women, a more severe postpartum depression may take hold of them, usually within four weeks of giving birth. A woman with postpartum depression may experience anxiety, panic attacks, and have trouble sleeping (unrelated to waking during the night to the sounds of a crying infant). She may cry for no apparent reason and show little interest in her baby. She may feel angry toward her baby and may appear agitated. For some women, the depression becomes so intense that they have thoughts about killing themselves or their children.

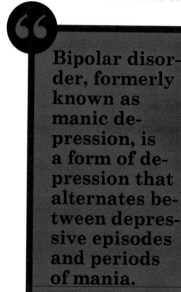

Bipolar disorder, formerly known as manic depression, is a form of depression that alternates between depressive episodes and periods of mania.

In some severe cases of postpartum depression, a woman may experience psychotic episodes such as delusions or hallucinations. She may believe that her baby is evil or magical. In extreme cases, the woman may try to harm or kill her child. "It's rare, but the symptoms are very severe. You start losing touch with what's real and imagined, you can have delusions and unpredictable actions,"[19] says Catherine Carlton, an advocate for awareness about postpartum depression.

According to the National Institute of Mental Health, 10 to 15 percent of women experience postpartum depression after the birth of a child. Women who experience postpartum depression are also more likely to experience a recurrence of depression with future births. "Women with postpartum depression need treatment with counseling and sometimes medication so that the depression does not become worse and last even longer,"[20] says Laura Schiller, an obstetrician and gynecologist in New York City.

## Bipolar Disorder

Bipolar disorder, formerly known as manic depression, is a form of depression that alternates between depressive episodes and periods of mania. More than normal ups and downs, bipolar disorder causes severe shifts in mood, energy, and activity levels. It can affect a person's ability to function in day-to-day life.

Bipolar disorder often develops during the late teens or in young adulthood. According to NIMH, at least half of people with bipolar disorder are diagnosed before age twenty-five. When symptoms begin, many people do not recognize them as part of an illness. Some suffer for years before they are diagnosed with the disorder. Bipolar disorder is a chronic disease that must be carefully managed for the rest of one's life.

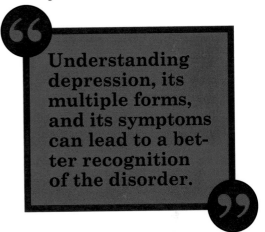

Understanding depression, its multiple forms, and its symptoms can lead to a better recognition of the disorder.

Actress and singer Demi Lovato was diagnosed with bipolar disorder in 2010. "I had no idea that I was even bipolar until I went into treatment," Lovato says. "I was actually manic a lot of the times that I would take on workloads, and I would say, 'Yes, I can do this, I can do this, I can do this.' I was conquering the world, but then I would come crashing down, and I would be more depressed than ever."[21]

## Depression Strikes

Depression can strike anyone, at any time. Frankie Sandford, a singer in the English girl band The Saturdays, has struggled with depression for most of her career. "Looking back, I realize it all started when I was about

15 or 16. . . . I used to stay in bed a lot; I had no motivation. I thought I was being lazy. And I think my parents just thought I was taking it easy, because I'd been working really hard,"[22] says Sandford.

As she worked over the years, Sandford fell into a cycle of performing, then coming home and going straight to bed, without having dinner or talking to anyone. She sought counseling for a time, but eventually stopped. By 2011, Sandford's depression began to spiral out of control. During a simple argument with her boyfriend, she became more upset than usual. "I managed to convince myself that he didn't know me at all. It set off this spiral of negative thinking—that if I disappeared, it wouldn't matter to anyone. In fact, it would make everybody's life easier. I felt that I was worthless, that I was ugly, that I didn't deserve anything,"[23] she says.

Sandford's depression continued to spiral downward, until the band's doctor convinced her to check into a hospital. There, Sandford participated in individual and group therapy. Eventually, she began to get better. "I'd noticed that I'd reached the end of the day without a panic attack, and without having two million conversations with myself about how terrible I was," she says. Today, Sandford takes each day at a time and says that most of the time her depression is under control. "I did lose myself, but I feel like me again now. But I try not to put pressure on myself—it's unrealistic, no one is happy 100% of the time,"[24] she says.

Depression is a complicated illness. The symptoms are different in each patient, and there are several forms of depression, making it difficult to diagnose. Still, understanding depression, its multiple forms, and its symptoms can lead to a better recognition of the disorder.

# Primary Source Quotes*

# What Are Depressive Disorders?

**Everyone experiences sadness from time to time; it is a normal part of life. Depression is when sadness goes on and is so severe it begins to interfere with your daily activities—your function in the world.**

—Kathi J. Kemper, "Can Depression Be Treated Naturally? An Interview with Kathi J. Kemper," *Nutrition Health Review: The Consumer's Medical Journal*, no. 102, 2010.

Kemper is the Caryl J. Guth Chair for the Center for Integrative Medicine at the Wake Forest University School of Medicine in North Carolina.

**Struggling against the enormous black waves of misery that kept trying to drown me in sorrow was the most difficult thing I have ever dealt with in my life.**

—Susan Polis Schutz, "Hearing Echoes of Optimism," *Esperanza*, Fall 2010.

Schutz is cofounder of Blue Mountain Arts publishing, and a depression patient.

* Editor's Note: While the definition of a primary source can be narrowly or broadly defined, for the purposes of Compact Research, a primary source consists of: 1) results of original research presented by an organization or researcher; 2) eyewitness accounts of events, personal experience, or work experience; 3) first-person editorials offering pundits' opinions; 4) government officials presenting political plans and/or policies; 5) representatives of organizations presenting testimony or policy.

Primary Source Quotes

**❝My mind felt foggy—like a hangover that never quits. Drugs didn't cause the grogginess; I only used a mild antidepressant. The haze in my brain felt permanent.❞**

—Julie Hersh, *Struck by Living: From Depression to Hope.* Austin, TX: Greenleaf, 2011.

Hersh is a depression patient and author.

........................................................................................................

**❝Many of the signs of depression are somatic: pain, fatigue, feeling stressed, insomnia.❞**

—Margaret Wehrenberg, *The 10 Best-Ever Depression Management Techniques.* New York: Norton, 2010.

Wehrenberg is a licensed psychologist, public speaker, and author.

........................................................................................................

**❝Bipolar disorder has been described as 'the worst hell imaginable,' and I could not agree more.❞**

—Genevieve Green, "Life Unlimited Stories: Genevieve Green," Depression and Bipolar Support Alliance, 2012. www.dbsalliance.org.

Green is a bipolar patient and winner of the 2012 International Bipolar Foundation's high school essay competition.

........................................................................................................

**❝It was as if I had suddenly had my brain replaced by someone weaker, angrier, sadder. . . . Though I didn't know it this was a dangerous and intense case of depression.❞**

—Linea Johnson, "Essay: Finding Dry Land," Depression and Bipolar Support Alliance, 2010. www.dbsalliance.org.

Johnson is a depression and bipolar patient from Seattle, Washington, and the coauthor of *Perfect Chaos*.

........................................................................................................

**❝Depression is a part of all of our lives. Everyone has experience with it either in their own families or with friends.❞**

—Jodie Foster, Q&A, "Ruminating Spirit: Jodie Foster on Depression, Healing and the Human Condition," *NAMI Advocate*, Winter 2011. www.nami.org.

Foster is an Academy Award–winning actress, director, and producer.

.......................................................................................................................................................

**❝One of the differences between depression and grief is time does help with grief. Depression is unrelenting.❞**

—Merely Me, "Grief and Mood Disorders: My Interview with Kay Redfield Jamison," *HealthCentral* (blog), February 1, 2010. www.healthcentral.com.

Merely Me is a blogger for *Health Central* and a depression patient.

.......................................................................................................................................................

## What Are Depressive Disorders?

- According to the Centers for Disease Control and Prevention, approximately 10 percent of people in the United States over the age of eighteen suffer from a depressive disorder.

- Major depressive disorder is the leading cause of disability among Americans aged fifteen to forty-four.

- The median age of onset for major depressive disorder is thirty-two, according to the National Institute of Mental Health.

- Women experience depression at twice the rate of men.

- According to the National Institute of Mental Health, symptoms of dysthymia must persist for at least two years in adults and one year in children to meet diagnostic criteria.

- According to the National Institute of Mental Health, dysthymia affects approximately 1.5 percent of the adult population in the United States.

- According to the Depression and Bipolar Support Alliance, as many as one in thirty-three children and one in eight adolescents have clinical depression.

# How Common Are Depressive Disorders?

The three most common depressive disorders—major depression, bipolar disorder, and dysthymia—affect approximately 23.8 million American adults each year. Major depression is the most common, affecting about one in fifteen American adults. Dysthymia, a milder, longer-lasting form of depression, is the least common of the three.

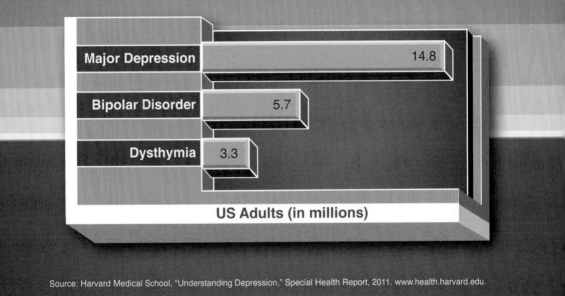

| | US Adults (in millions) |
|---|---|
| Major Depression | 14.8 |
| Bipolar Disorder | 5.7 |
| Dysthymia | 3.3 |

Source: Harvard Medical School, "Understanding Depression," Special Health Report, 2011. www.health.harvard.edu.

- According to the Cleveland Clinic, between 4 and 6 percent of the US population suffer from seasonal affective disorder.

- Three-quarters of seasonal affective disorder patients are women, most of whom are in their twenties, thirties, and forties, according to the Cleveland Clinic.

- A depressive episode, left untreated, can last six months or may become chronic, according to Families for Depression Awareness.

## Depression by Age

Depression affects people of all ages. According to the National Institute of Mental Health, the average age of onset of major depression is in the mid-twenties. By the time a person turns eighteen years old, there is one in ten likelihood he or she will develop depression.

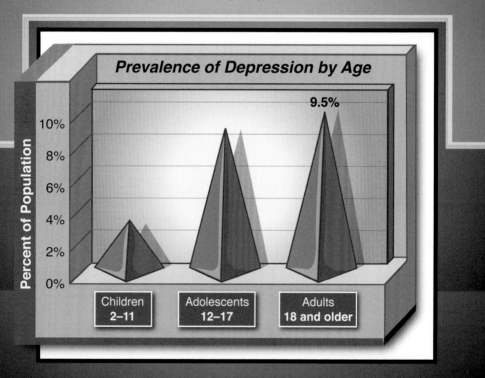

**Prevalence of Depression by Age**

Source: Aalok Mehta, "Depression: Making a Difference Tomorrow," BrainFacts.org, January 1, 2011. www.brainfacts.org.

- The National Institute of Mental Health estimates that 10 to 15 percent of women experience postpartum depression after giving birth.

- According to All About Depression, a depression support and resource organization, psychotic symptoms occur in postpartum mothers in about one out of every five hundred to one thousand births.

# What Causes Depressive Disorders?

**"Still mysterious is how drugs, stress, or other experiences can engender longer-term effects, causing an individual to succumb to depression or addiction."**

—Eric Nestler, Nash Family Professor of Neuroscience and director of the Friedman Brain Institute at the Mount Sinai Medical Center in New York City.

**"Not everyone gets depressed or anxious. There's a complex interplay between genetics, hormones, other biological goings-on and the contexts of the paths we take in our lives."**

—Kathleen M. Hegadoren, Canada Research Chair in Stress-Related Disorders in Women, University of Alberta.

There is no simple answer to what causes depression. Depression can strike people of any age, gender, race, or social background. Most experts believe that a combination of genetic, biological, and environmental factors interact to influence whether someone develops depression. Yet the complexity of the brain along with the varied effects that depression can have on thoughts, feelings, and behaviors make the disorder a challenge to study. According to a Harvard Medical School Special Health Report, "Depression has many possible causes, including genetic vulnerability, stressful life events, and faulty mood regulation by the brain. . . . With this level of complexity, you can see how two people might have similar symptoms of depression, but the problem on the inside, and therefore what treatments will work best, may be entirely different."[25]

While having a risk factor may increase a person's chances of developing depression, it does not mean a person will indeed develop it. Many people with risk factors for depression never develop it. Yet research has shown that the more risk factors a person has, the greater chance he or she has of becoming depressed. Knowing the risk factors can help a person recognize whether he or she is vulnerable to depression. With this knowledge, the person can learn about the disease, its warning signs, and treatments.

# Gender

As children, boys and girls develop depression at equal rates. When girls reach adolescence, however, their likelihood of becoming depressed increases. The National Alliance on Mental Illness reports that by the time they become adults, women are twice as likely as men to develop major depression.

The reason women suffer more from depression is unknown. Many experts believe that women are more vulnerable because of frequent changes in hormone levels related to menstruation, pregnancy, and menopause. Another possible factor may be the increased stress women face from balancing work and family life. A 2011 European research study reported that women between the ages of twenty-five and forty were three to four times more likely to become depressed than men. "In females, you see these incredibly high rates of depressive episodes at times when they sometimes have their babies, where they raise children, where they have to cope with the double responsibility of job and family,"[26] says Professor Hans Ulrich Wittchen, one of the study's lead authors from the Dresden University of Technology in Germany.

# Family History

Research on depression in families shows that people have a higher chance of developing the disorder if a parent or sibling also has depression. Having a close relative with major depression makes a person one-and-a-half to three times more likely to develop the illness. For bipolar disorder, the family connection is even stronger. According to the National Institute of Mental Health, children with a parent or sibling who has bipolar disorder are four to six times more likely to develop the illness. Having a close relative with bipolar disorder also increases the chances of a person's developing major depression.

Because of the family connection, researchers believe that genes may play a role, and they are attempting to identify specific genes that may cause depression. In 2011, researchers from the University of Michigan reported finding evidence that people with a particular gene were more likely to develop depression when faced with stressful life events. This gene prevented study participants from reabsorbing mood-regulating serotonin into the brain's nerve cells. "It gives a very clear answer: the 'short' variant of the serotonin transporter does make people more sensitive to the effects of adversity,"[27] says Rudolf Uher, a clinical lecturer at the Institute of Psychiatry at King's College London.

> **Most experts believe that a combination of genetic, biological, and environmental factors interact to influence whether someone develops depression.**

In two separate studies, researchers from King's College London and Washington University in St. Louis reported in 2011 that they had found a stretch of chromosome 3 that was associated with depression. "In a large number of families where two or more members have depression, we found robust evidence that a region [of chromosome 3] called 3p25-26 is strongly linked to the disorder," says Gerome Breen, lead author of the King's College study. "These findings are truly exciting as possibly for the first time we have found a genetic locus for depression."[28] Researchers plan to conduct further research to identify the gene within that region that plays a role in depression.

Still, much work remains to understand how genes influence depression. Scientists believe that more than one hundred genes may contribute to depression. In addition, researchers still believe that other factors, such as environment and brain chemistry, also influence who develops depression. This may explain why many people who inherit a gene linked to depression do not develop the disorder. "Most people with the gene—even when stressed—do not develop depression," says Gary Kennedy, director of the Division of Geriatric Psychiatry at Montefiore Medical Center in New York City, so "the associated risk is real but very small."[29]

## Personal History

Having a previous depressive episode can make a person more vulnerable to future episodes. According to the National Alliance on Mental Illness, more than half of people with untreated major depression will have a second depressive episode. With each additional depressive episode, a person's risk of recurrence further increases.

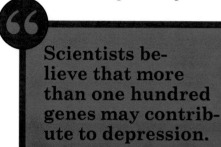

> Scientists believe that more than one hundred genes may contribute to depression.

Having one depressive disorder also increases a person's risk for developing another form of depression. People with dysthymia have an increased risk of developing major depression. As many as 80 to 90 percent will get major depression, says David J. Hellerstein, professor of clinical psychiatry at Columbia University and a research psychiatrist at New York State Psychiatric Institute. "It's like if you have asthma, you are more likely to get bronchitis and pneumonia because you have this baseline condition all the time,"[30] he says.

## Brain Structure and Function

Certain areas of the human brain regulate mood. Researchers believe that differences in brain structure and how the brain works may be factors in determining who develops depression. Sophisticated brain imaging such as positron emission tomography (PET) and functional magnetic resonance imaging (fMRI) allow researchers to look closely at the working brain. Using this technology, researchers can see the changes that take place in the brain during different tasks or situations. Brain imaging shows that the brains of people with depression look different from the brains of those without the illness. In particular, the parts of the brain that regulate mood, thinking, sleep, appetite, and behavior appear to function improperly. For example, research has found that people with thinning of tissue in the brain's right hemisphere may have a greater risk of depression.

How the brain's structures are connected and interact with each other may also play a role in depression. In a 2012 study, researchers from the Semel Institute for Neuroscience and Human Behavior at the University of California in Los Angeles (UCLA) reported that people with depression appear to have hyperactive brain activity. The study measured the synchronization of the brain's electrical signals and studied the functional connections among the different brain regions. "All the depressed patients showed increased connectivity," says Andrew Leuchter, UCLA psychiatry professor and lead author of the study. "We know from brain science studying normal individuals that the connections are turning off and on all the time. If you take a snapshot of a depressed person's brain, you're going to find the connections turned on at any given time."[31] The depressed brain is able to form functional connections but appears to lose its ability to turn the connections off, says Leuchter. This may cause some of the mental and emotional symptoms of depression such as low mood and difficulty concentrating. "This inability to control how brain areas work together may help explain some of the symptoms in depression,"[32] he says.

> " Research indicates that people with depression have neurotransmitter imbalances. "

## Brain Chemicals and Hormones

Brain chemistry appears to play a significant role in depression. Neurotransmitters are chemicals that send messages across gaps, called synapses, between the brain's nerve cells, or neurons. Neurotransmitters affect how a person feels, thinks, and behaves. Research indicates that people with depression have neurotransmitter imbalances. These imbalances can cause the messages from the brain to the body to be mixed up or not delivered. When this happens, depressive symptoms may occur.

Two neurotransmitters linked to depression are serotonin and norepinephrine. Serotonin helps to regulate sleep, appetite, and mood. Some studies suggest that decreased serotonin levels may lead to depression. Low levels of norepinephrine have been connected to fatigue and depressed mood. Other neurotransmitters that may play a role in depression include acetylcholine, dopamine, glutamate, and gamma-aminobutyric acid, or GABA.

Problems with hormone levels may also play a role in depression. One hormone that has been linked to depression is cortisol. The body's adrenal glands make cortisol in response to stress. Research has shown that about 50 percent of people with depression also have high levels of cortisol in their blood. When the person's depressive symptoms disappear, high cortisol levels generally return to normal.

In women, scientists are also studying the effect that cyclical changes in hormones such as estrogen have on brain chemistry and depression. The significant life changes that women go through during puberty, menstruation, pregnancy, and menopause are associated with fluctuations in hormones. Researchers have found that these hormonal changes lead to increased risk of depression. For example, in a 2010 study from the University of Pittsburgh, researchers found that an increase in testosterone levels during perimenopause (the period just before true menopause) and menopause was significantly associated with depressive symptoms.

## Stress and Trauma Triggers

Everyone experiences stressful life events at some point: the death of a loved one, a divorce, or the loss of a job. Traumatic events such as the murder of a loved one or a serious accident can cause high levels of stress. Even happy events like a new job or marriage can cause stress. While everyone experiences stress, reactions to it can differ greatly. For those vulnerable to depression, the combination of stressful events, genetics, and biology may trigger depression.

Although stress can trigger depression in some people, it does not affect all people in the same way. Not everyone who becomes depressed has experienced high levels of stress. In addition, the same stressful event may trigger depression in one person but not in another. Those who struggle with chronic depression might develop a sensitivity to stress. For these people, even small stresses can lead to deeper depression.

## Childhood Events

Experiencing losses or trauma as a child can have a significant effect on a person's risk of developing depression. These events include physical, sexual, or verbal abuse; separation from a parent; an unstable home; or a parent's mental illness. In fact, the death of a parent before a child reaches age eleven is the event most significantly linked to depression.

Throughout most of her teen years, Donna, a college student, has struggled with depression. She believes her condition may have been triggered by childhood physical abuse. In one incident, Donna remembers that her father "proceeded to whip me severely with his belt. He slapped me, grabbed me by the neck and tossed me around his room. The beating lasted for what seemed like centuries. . . . I remember going back to my room and sitting on the ground in pain . . . unsure of what had just happened. That was the first time I truly ever considered suicide."[33]

> **Experiencing losses or trauma as a child can have a significant effect on a person's risk of developing depression.**

According to research published in the *American Journal of Psychiatry* in 2011, people who experienced maltreatment as children were twice as likely to develop multiple and long-lasting depressive episodes as those who were not maltreated. Researchers from the King's College London Institute of Psychiatry also reported that those maltreated as children were less likely to respond to treatment for depression. Previous studies have shown children who are maltreated are more likely to have abnormalities in the brain and endocrine systems, areas that deal with stress. "The results indicate that childhood maltreatment is associated both with an increased risk of developing recurrent and persistent episodes of depression, and with an increased risk of responding poorly to treatment,"[34] says Andrea Danese, senior investigator of the study at King's College London.

## Many Factors

Depression is a medical illness; yet unlike other illnesses, it is not always easy to identify and treat because it is not caused by a single factor. Instead, a combination of genetic, biological, and environmental factors appear to be involved in causing depression.

Every person reacts differently to depression's risk factors. The same conditions may cause some to fall into a deep depression while others still function normally. Although it is difficult to identify the exact cause of depression, understanding risk factors may help a person be more aware of warning signs and thus be able to make life changes that reduce the risks.

## Primary Source Quotes*

# What Causes Depressive Disorders?

66 Like most common medical conditions, these neurological afflictions are highly heritable: roughly half the risk for addiction or depression is genetic—which is greater than the genetic risk for high blood pressure or most cancers. 99

—Eric Nestler, "Hidden Switches in the Mind," *Scientific American*, December 2011.

Nestler is the Nash Family Professor of Neuroscience and director of the Friedman Brain Institute at the Mount Sinai Medical Center in New York City.

66 The catalyst for depressive episodes can vary, but it's generally accepted that stress associated with major life changes can coax the sleeping black dog from his cozy den. 99

—Bruce Clark, "Fighting for Self-Awareness," *Esperanza*, Fall 2010.

Clark is a writer and stand-up comedian who was diagnosed with depression in his early thirties.

* Editor's Note: While the definition of a primary source can be narrowly or broadly defined, for the purposes of Compact Research, a primary source consists of: 1) results of original research presented by an organization or researcher; 2) eyewitness accounts of events, personal experience, or work experience; 3) first-person editorials offering pundits' opinions; 4) government officials presenting political plans and/or policies; 5) representatives of organizations presenting testimony or policy.

Primary Source Quotes

**❝I had had enough bouts of depression to virtually assure I would have more. It seems that the physiological ruts in my brain, layered on an apparent genetic predisposition toward depression, had sealed my fate.❞**

—Vincent Caimano, "In Charge of Change," *Esperanza*, Summer 2011.

Caimano is the founder of Depression Recovery Groups and himself a depression patient.

........................................................................................

**❝Although depression is a common mental-health complaint and a leading cause of disability over the course of a lifetime, it is hard to understand what causes it and how to treat it.❞**

—Margaret Wehrenberg, *The 10 Best-Ever Depression Management Techniques*. New York: Norton, 2010.

Wehrenberg is a licensed psychologist, public speaker, and author.

........................................................................................

**❝Adolescence is the time when we see depressive symptoms escalate, particularly in girls.❞**

—Karen Kochel, "Study: Adolescents Suffering from Depression More Likely to Be Bullied," Arizona State University, February 8, 2012. https://clas.asu.edu.

Kochel is an assistant research professor at Arizona State University's School of Social and Family Dynamics.

........................................................................................

**❝If we understand the underlying physiological abnormalities contributing to mood disorders, then we are likely to benefit from more effective solutions.❞**

—James M. Greenblatt, "The Brain on Fire: Inflammation and Depression," *Psychology Today*, November 23, 2011. http://www.psychologytoday.com.

Greenblatt is a psychiatrist who treats children and adults.

........................................................................................

**❝Stress plays an important role in depression.❞**

—Harvard Medical School, "Understanding Depression," Special Health Report, 2011. www.health.harvard.edu.

Harvard Health Publications are published by the Harvard University Medical School.

---

**❝If you're depressed, it might not be easy to figure out why. In most cases, depression doesn't have a single cause. Instead, it results from a mix of things—your genes, events in your past, your current circumstances, and other risk factors.❞**

—WebMD, "Recognizing and Treating Depression: Common Causes of Depression," 2012. www.webmd.com.

WebMD is an online source that provides information on a variety of health and medical topics.

---

# Facts and Illustrations

## What Causes Depressive Disorders?

- According to the World Health Organization, **50 to 75 percent** of children are likely to suffer from depression if both parents also have the illness.

- Depression is associated with physical illness. **Twenty-five percent** of cancer patients also have depression, according to the Depression and Bipolar Support Alliance.

- Studies show **80 to 90 percent** of those who suffer from bipolar disorder have relatives with some form of depression, according to Mental Health America.

- Some studies suggest that women who experience **postpartum depression** often have had prior depressive episodes, according to the National Alliance on Mental Illness.

- According to the American Academy of Child & Adolescent Psychiatry, research suggests that if one identical twin has bipolar disorder, there is an approximately **70 percent** chance that the other twin will eventually develop the illness.

- According to the support group All About Depression, the most significant **traumatic event** linked to depression in children is a long separation from or death of a parent before the child's eleventh birthday.

## Adverse Childhood Experiences Increase Risk of Depression

Early childhood events have a strong influence on children. According to the Substance Abuse and Mental Health Services Administration, women who have been exposed to traumatic childhood events, such as abuse or the death of a parent, are more likely to experience a depressive disorder than other women. As the number of adverse events increases, so does the person's risk of depression.

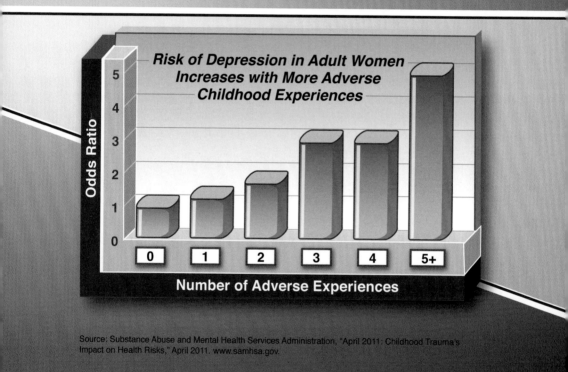

**Risk of Depression in Adult Women Increases with More Adverse Childhood Experiences**

Odds Ratio

Number of Adverse Experiences

Source: Substance Abuse and Mental Health Services Administration, "April 2011: Childhood Trauma's Impact on Health Risks," April 2011. www.samhsa.gov.

- If a person experiences a single episode of depression, there is a **50 percent** chance of having another. The chance of recurrence is **70 percent** after two episodes and **90 percent** after three episodes, states Families for Depression Awareness.

# Brain Structure and Function Influence Depression Risk

Certain areas of the brain regulate mood. Sophisticated brain imaging techniques allow researchers to look closely at the working brain and observe how brain structure is different in people with depression. Areas that appear to have a significant role in depression are the amygdala, the basal ganglia, the prefrontal cortex, the thalamus, and the hippocampus. Researchers are investigating how structural changes, as well as changes in blood flow and activity in these areas, relate to depression risk.

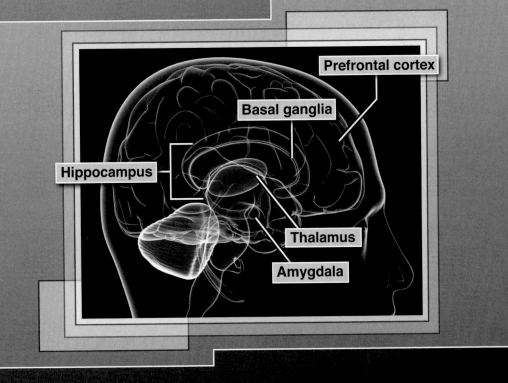

Source: Harvard Medical School, "Understanding Depression," Special Health Report, 2011. www.health.harvard.edu.

- About **50 percent** of people with clinical depression have an excess of the hormone cortisol in their blood.

**66Depression affects how we make decisions, respond to events and interactions, feel about successes and failures, affecting everything we do from the time we wake up until the time we go to sleep.99**

—Dennis Greenberger, clinical psychologist and coauthor of *Mind over Mood: Change How You Feel by Changing the Way You Think.*

**66I don't know when I will crawl out of it, but crawl out of it I will. I've learned as a man who suffers [from] bipolar disorder that there will be good days and there will be bad days. I have to prosper when it's good and keep the damage to a bare minimum when things aren't so hot.99**

—Tim McGhee, bipolar disorder patient.

Depressive disorders can affect a person's life in many ways. They impair a person's ability to sleep, eat, and work. They damage relationships with family and friends. Depressed people often feel bad about themselves and experience a vicious cycle of self-doubt that lowers self-esteem and confidence. In addition, being depressed can lead to unhealthy behaviors like eating disorders, substance abuse, and self-injury.

CNN journalist Kat Kinsman was diagnosed with depression as a teenager. She remembers how depression made it difficult to do even the simplest daily tasks. She recalls:

> I am 14 years old, it's the middle of the afternoon, and I'm curled into a ball at the bottom of the stairs. I've intended to drag my uncooperative limbs upstairs to my dark disaster of a bedroom and sleep until everything hurts a little less, but my body and brain have simply drained down. I crumple into a bony, frizzy-haired heap on the gold shag rug, convinced that the only thing I have left to offer the world is the removal of my ugly presence from it, but at that moment, I'm too exhausted to do anything about it.[35]

## Physical Effects

Depression is a mental illness that also affects people physically. During a depressive episode, people may experience changes in appetite, sleep patterns, and energy levels. It is difficult to predict how depression will affect each person. Some people may be hungry all the time, while others lose their appetite. Some people find that they are tired all the time and sleep more than usual. Others develop insomnia and spend hours awake.

Depression can also cause headaches, stomachaches, back pain, and other chronic aches and pains. At first, thirty-nine-year-old Dichelle Connell from Charlotte, North Carolina, thought she had the flu. She felt exhausted, had a headache, and her muscles ached. After a few weeks, she still did not feel any better and had added a sinus infection to her list of ailments. "I was as sick as a dog and had no idea what was wrong,"[36] recalls Connell. A round of antibiotics prescribed by her doctor did little to help ease her symptoms. Her eye developed a twitch that was severe enough to cause difficulty driving and watching television, yet doctors could find no medical cause. Finally,

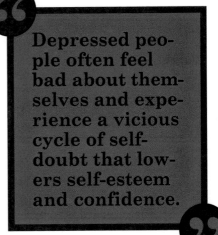

Depressed people often feel bad about themselves and experience a vicious cycle of self-doubt that lowers self-esteem and confidence.

when Connell mentioned her array of symptoms to her psychologist, he suggested that they might all be linked to depression. Just before her physical symptoms began, Connell had suffered several miscarriages. Her therapist suggested that her body might be responding to the trauma in her life. Connell concurred: "It made complete sense to me when I started thinking about it. If your brain is responding to some sort of trauma, it makes sense that your body will, too."[37]

## Emotional Impact

People with depression frequently feel that their emotions are out of control. They might experience extreme sadness or they might find that their anger erupts at the smallest annoyance. Beth-Sarah Wright, a thirty-seven-year-old Atlanta college professor, did her best to hide her intense emotional swings. Often, bouts of overwhelming sadness would hit her while in the middle of teaching a class. She would excuse herself from the classroom and seek an empty hallway or bathroom. Alone, Wright would sob uncontrollably. After a few minutes, she would pull herself back together and return to her students. "I wore a powerful mask," she says. "I could put on a riveting performance, both in the classroom and at home."[38]

Depression can also make people feel emotionally distant. Says Safa, a teenager diagnosed with depression, "I very quickly began to feel distant and in a world of my own from my classmates who were always laughing and smiling. . . . I withdrew myself completely from the friends I once had, my family—everyone. I didn't think anyone understood me. I savoured solitude."[39]

## Cognitive Effect

Depression can affect how an individual thinks. People with depression may find it harder to think normally when they are depressed. Some people report that they feel as if their brain is fuzzy. They may have trouble remembering details, concentrating, and paying attention. Some people find they have difficulty making a decision and sticking with it. These cognitive problems can interfere with a person's performance at work or school. People in intellectually demanding jobs such as engineers or doctors may suddenly find themselves unable to perform. For children and teens, cognitive problems may affect their grades at school.

Lauren is a PhD student who was diagnosed with depression. She says that her depression made it difficult to think and function in her demanding postgraduate program. "The best way I can describe the way I felt during this time is that my brain was scrambled, as if it was full of noisy wool so I couldn't think about anything other than how stressed I felt; I couldn't think about my work, read books or even listen to other people when they were talking to me," she says. "As a postgraduate research student I'm basically supposed to be in my office all day every day, but I was finding it impossible to concentrate for long enough to get anywhere."[40]

## Negative Thoughts

People with depression have persistent, often uncontrollable negative thoughts about themselves, the world, the people around them, and the future. They may dwell on past mistakes and blame themselves for things that are not their fault.

For people with depression, negative thinking can quickly spiral out of control. "Habitual negative thinking can lead to many problems," says Simon Rego, director of psychology training at Montefiore Medical Center and assistant professor of psychiatry and behavioral sciences at Albert Einstein College of Medicine in New York City. "First, given the connection between thoughts and emotions, [negative thoughts] can serve to bring down or keep down your mood. Second, negative thoughts can influence the way you act and react, which can lead to a variety of problematic behaviors."[41]

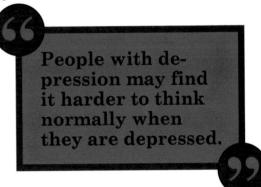

> People with depression may find it harder to think normally when they are depressed.

Many depressed people find it hard to stop the destructive spiral of negative thinking. Over time, negative thoughts can become a normal part of their everyday thought processes. "Often the negative thinking becomes habitual as a defense mechanism to rationalize the feelings of depression," says Forrest Hong, a psychologist and social worker in Los Angeles. "After awhile, these negative behaviors seem like an easier technique of coping with depression symptoms."[42]

## Risky Behavior

Many depressed people feel they cannot cope with their feelings of depression. To escape, they might engage in risky behaviors. Getting into fights, using drugs and alcohol, sexual promiscuity, and self-injury are all signs that a person may be in a serious depression.

A study published in *Journal Watch: Pediatrics and Adolescent Medicine* in March 2012 supports the link between depression and risky behavior. Researchers followed forty-four hundred high school students for several years and found that adolescents with higher levels of depressive symptoms were more likely to report cigarette smoking, marijuana use, and hard-drug use as compared with teens having lower levels of depressive symptoms. These findings add to concerns about substance abuse in people who suffer from depression.

## Damage to Relationships

Depression often causes people to act in unusual ways around family and friends, at work, and at school. They may cry easily or become quickly irritated. While depressed, a patient may withdraw from family and friends. Activities that once interested them no longer hold any appeal. Their erratic behavior and mood swings can cause problems in interpersonal relationships.

> Getting into fights, using drugs and alcohol, sexual promiscuity, and self-injury are all signs a person may be in a serious depression.

As Beth-Sarah Wright's depression deepened, she began to lash out at her husband. She would take out her anger and frustration by screaming at him. "At first my fits of rage would be out of earshot of my children," she says. "But eventually they heard me . . . go off on their father for no reason. It was a very, very stressful and confusing time for all of us."[43] Eventually, Wright's depression put a serious strain on her relationship with her husband. He suggested that they see a marriage counselor.

Close family members and friends are often intensely affected by a patient's depression. Research shows that when a person has depression, there is a significant impact on the well-being of his or her partner. According to research from the Norwegian Institute of Public Health published in August 2010, spouses of people with mental illness, including depression, were likely to show signs of anxiety and depression themselves. "Depression doesn't just impact the person with the diagnosis, it impacts their [partner], too,"[44] says Lynne Knobloch-Fedders, a licensed clinical psychologist and director of research at the Family Institute at Northwestern University.

> For some depressed people, life becomes so unbearable and hopeless that they think the only way to stop the pain is to end their life.

Catherine, a sixty-five-year-old nurse from Vancouver, British Columbia, married her husband, James, in 2003, knowing his history of depression. For years, the couple managed to cope with James's mild depressive episodes and symptoms; however, when James's father passed away and he lost his job in the same year, he fell into a deep depression. Catherine discovered that the husband and life she had known for years had suddenly disappeared. "We lost all of the things we used to do together," says Catherine. "Our life became much smaller. I was getting worn down and didn't know how to cope. It affected him, me and our relationship."[45]

## High Risk of Suicide

For some depressed people, life becomes so unbearable and hopeless that they think the only way to stop the pain is to end their life. According to the American Foundation for Suicide Prevention, at least 90 percent of people who kill themselves have a psychiatric illness such as major depression, bipolar disorder, or another depressive illness. In addition, a person's risk of suicide increases if his or her depression is untreated. In fact, untreated depression is the number one risk for suicide among youth.

According to the Centers for Disease Control and Prevention (CDC), someone in the United States dies by suicide every fifteen minutes. Many more think about, plan, or attempt to kill themselves. People are more likely to attempt suicide if they have a previous history of suicide attempts, abuse alcohol or drugs, have a family history of suicide or violence, or have a serious physical illness.

Legendary journalist and *60 Minutes* correspondent Mike Wallace suffered for years with depression. At his lowest point, Wallace said, suicide seemed like the only way out. In the midst of a major bout of depression in the 1980s, Wallace found himself feeling dead inside. He had no appetite and took sleeping pills to cope with insomnia. He consulted a family doctor who reassured him that he could just "get through it." Yet the depression continued to consume him, and he decided to end his life. "I have to get out of here," he remembers thinking. "So I took a bunch of sleeping pills, wrote a note and ate them, and, as a result, I fell asleep."[46] Wallace's wife found him unconscious in bed and alerted doctors. After his recovery Wallace began talk therapy and antidepressant medication to manage his depression. Although he suffered more depressive episodes over the years, Wallace said that getting treatment helped him better cope with his illness.

## A Productive Life with Depression

Despite having to deal with the physical, emotional, cognitive, and social effects of depression, many people are able to live normal and productive lives. Some very successful people have been diagnosed and treated for depression, including sports stars, actors, writers, and politicians. The list includes actress Angelina Jolie, Olympic skating star Dorothy Hamill, singer Sheryl Crow, rocker Pete Wentz, astronaut Buzz Aldrin, and baseball player Zack Greinke. These people and many others show it is possible to cope with depression and live a successful, productive life.

# Primary Source Quotes*

# How Do Depressive Disorders Affect People?

66 **Bipolars are, at the least, annoying to those close to them. The mood swings influence the person's inability to live in the real world and make wise real world decisions.** 99

—Tim McGhee, "Sports and Mental Illness: How Bipolar Disorder Can Affect Athletic Performance," Bleacher Report, December 28, 2010. http://bleacherreport.com.

McGhee is a correspondent for the sports website Bleacher Report and suffers from bipolar disorder.

66 **I have pathetically low self-esteem which fuels my chronic major depression.** 99

—Michael Rafferty, "Losing a Job, Gaining Perspective," *Esperanza*, Fall 2010.

Rafferty suffers from major depression.

* Editor's Note: While the definition of a primary source can be narrowly or broadly defined, for the purposes of Compact Research, a primary source consists of: 1) results of original research presented by an organization or researcher; 2) eyewitness accounts of events, personal experience, or work experience; 3) first-person editorials offering pundits' opinions; 4) government officials presenting political plans and/or policies; 5) representatives of organizations presenting testimony or policy.

Primary Source Quotes

❝I came to feel more and more that my illness was an inescapable part of my identity. Anxiety and depression tunneled deeper into my very core.❞

—Jenny Stamos, "Looking Past the Label," *Esperanza*, Fall 2010.

Stamos has dysthymia.

---

❝I became frustrated easily and I could feel the anger I had caged up deep inside escaping from the metaphoric bars now weakened by the depression.❞

—Bruce Clark, "Fighting for Self-Awareness," *Esperanza*, Fall 2010.

Clark is a writer and stand-up comedian who was diagnosed with depression in his early thirties.

---

❝Because depression has the potential to undermine the maturation of key developmental skills, such as establishing healthy peer relationships, it's important to be aware of the signs and symptoms of adolescent depression.❞

—Karen Kochel, "Study: Adolescents Suffering from Depression More Likely to Be Bullied," Arizona State University, February 8, 2012. https://clas.asu.edu.

Kochel is an assistant research professor in Arizona State University's School of Social and Family Dynamics.

---

❝At the deepest point of despair, pain killed language. There were no words left. Only the brilliant lights and the painful darkness that characterized my depression were left.❞

—Laura Droege, "Shadows and Light," in Alise Wright, ed., *Not Alone: Stories of Living with Depression*. Folsom, CA: Civitas, 2011.

Droege is an aspiring author who suffers from bipolar disorder.

---

**❝Depression numbs me, buries me alive inside a glass casket—I am screaming but nobody hears.❞**

> —Elizabeth Esther, "Foreword," in Alise Wright, ed., *Not Alone: Stories of Living with Depression.* Folsom, CA: Civitas, 2011.

Esther is an author and blogger who has struggled with depression.

.........................................................................................

**❝Depression can have enormous depths and staying power. . . . You may find that you can't sleep or eat, that you are fatigued, or that you have headaches or aches and pains that seem to have sprung up without a cause.❞**

> —Harvard Medical School, "Understanding Depression," Special Health Report, 2011. www.health.harvard.edu.

Harvard Medical School's Special Health Reports are published by Harvard Health Publications.

.........................................................................................

# Facts and Illustrations

## How Do Depressive Disorders Affect People?

- More than **90 percent** of people who kill themselves have a diagnosable mental disorder, most commonly a depressive disorder or a substance abuse disorder, according to the National Institute of Mental Health.

- Untreated depression is the number one risk for **suicide among youth**, according to the Depression and Bipolar Support Alliance.

- Depressive disorders often co-occur with **anxiety disorders** and **substance abuse**.

- People with depression are four times as likely to have a **heart attack** as those without a history of depression, reports the Depression and Bipolar Support Alliance.

- According to the Medical College of Wisconsin, **50 percent** of Parkinson's disease patients may also experience depression.

- According to the Depression and Bipolar Support Alliance, **27 percent** of individuals with substance abuse disorders also are clinically depressed.

- According to a Harvard Medical School study, each US worker with bipolar disorder averaged **65.5 lost workdays** in a year, compared with 27.2 days for major depression.

# Drug Abuse and Depression

Many people with depression exhibit risky behavior while dealing with their illness. Many turn to illicit drugs to help them cope with symptoms. According to a government report, young people between the ages of twelve and seventeen who experienced a major depressive episode in the previous year were almost twice as likely to use illicit drugs as youth who did not have a depressive episode.

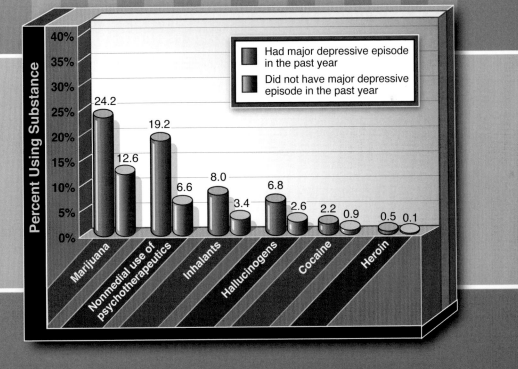

Source: *SAMSHA News*, "Mental Health Statistics on Youth," November/December 2010. www.samhsa.gov.

- According to SAVE.org, **15 percent** of those who are clinically depressed die by suicide.

- The National Alliance on Mental Health says that the **unemployment rate** for people living with mental illness, including depression, is three to five times higher than for those without mental illness.

# Depression Affects Daily Life

Clinical depression is a debilitating condition affecting every aspect of a person's life. In a 2012 report, teens and young adults who have experienced a major depressive episode state that it impaired their lives in three areas; work, relationships, and social life. Most respondents reported that the effects ranged from mild to severe, with some experiencing very severe effects and relatively few experiencing no effects at all.

## Severity of Impairment Due to Symptoms of Depression Among Persons Aged 18 to 22 with Past Year Major Depressive Episode (MDE), by Full-Time College Status: Percentages, 2008 to 2010

| Severity of Impairment | Full-Time College Students (%) | Other Young Adults (%) |
|---|---|---|
| Ability to Work: No Interference | 6% | 6.5% |
| Ability to Work: Mild | 31.4% | 28.5% |
| Ability to Work: Moderate | 39.9% | 38.1% |
| Ability to Work: Severe | 19.2% | 20.5% |
| Ability to Work: Very Severe | 3.5% | 6.4% |
| Close Relationships: No Interference | 2.7% | 2.4% |
| Close Relationships: Mild | 19.4% | 18.3% |
| Close Relationships: Moderate | 31.6% | 33.4% |
| Close Relationships: Severe | 38% | 32.9% |
| Close Relationships: Very Severe | 8.2% | 13% |
| Social Life: No Interference | 3.1% | 3.7% |
| Social Life: Mild | 16.9% | 15% |
| Social Life: Moderate | 32.2% | 35.8% |
| Social Life: Severe | 39.2% | 32.2% |
| Social Life: Very Severe | 8.6% | 13.3% |

Source: Substance Abuse and Mental Health Services Administration, Center for Behavioral Health Statistics and Quality, NSDUH Report: Major Depressive Episode Among Full-Time College Students and Other Young Adults, Aged 18 to 22, May 3, 2012. www.samhsa.gov.

## Adults with Depression More Likely to Smoke

Depression affects people in many ways, including how they behave and the choices they make. People with depression are more likely to engage in unhealthy behavior, as an escape from the pressure of dealing with their disease. According to a report from the National Center for Health Statistics, adults with depression were more likely to be cigarette smokers (43 percent) than adults without depression (22 percent). As depression severity increased, the percentage of adults who were smokers increased as well.

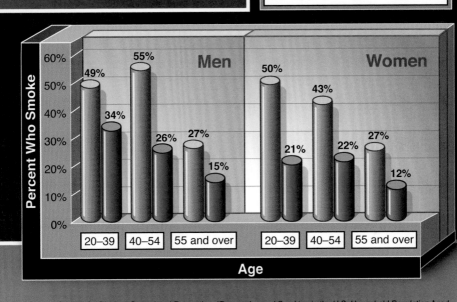

Source: Centers for Disease Control and Prevention, "Depression and Smoking in the U.S. Household Population Aged 20 and Over, 2005–2008," NCHS Data Brief, no. 34, April 2010. www.cdc.gov.

- One in four people with **cancer** also suffers from major depression.

- The National Alliance on Mental Illness estimates that approximately one-third to one-half of people with a serious mental illness, including depression, live at or near the **federal poverty level**.

- According to a survey by the Depression Alliance, **32 percent** of people with depression believed that they had been turned down for a job because of their depression.

# What Treatments Are Available for Depressive Disorders?

**"This wasn't like trying to rehab my injured knee. By attempting to push through on my own, I was only deepening my depression. I didn't get on the road to true recovery until I started being honest with myself and others and admitted that I was vulnerable—that this was one thing I couldn't defeat by myself."**

—Chamique Holdsclaw, WNBA player.

**"We need better treatments, not simply more of the same. If we are to start to contain depression, the public needs to demand them and to agree to fund the research that will bring them into being."**

—Jonathan Rottenberg, associate professor of psychology at the University of South Florida and director of the university's Mood and Emotion Laboratory.

D epression, even in its most severe form, is a treatable illness. Up to 80 percent of patients see an improvement in their symptoms within four to six weeks of beginning treatment. For some, the first depressive episode will be their last. For others, depression will return at a future date. For this reason, early diagnosis and treatment of depression is very important. The earlier treatment begins the more effective it can be at preventing a recurrence of symptoms and reducing risky behaviors that some people use to cope with depression. For most people, treatment for depressive disorders involves talk therapy, medication, or a combination of the two.

Left untreated, depressive disorders can last for years. Approximately half of those who have a single untreated episode of major depression will have another. Every untreated episode increases the risk for future occurrences that will likely be both more frequent and more severe.

## Talk Therapy

Talk therapy, or psychotherapy, is a common treatment for depression. It aims to relieve people's depressive symptoms and help them manage their problems better. Talk therapy can take place in individual, group, or family sessions. During a session, the patient talks to an expert about his or her feelings and problems and learns strategies to deal with them. According to the American Psychological Association, talk therapy can help patients "pinpoint the life problems that contribute to their depression, and help them understand which aspects of those problems they may be able to solve or improve."[47]

The most common types of talk therapy to treat depression are cognitive behavioral therapy (CBT), interpersonal therapy (IPT), and psychodynamic therapy. CBT is based on the idea that people's thoughts influence their feelings and behaviors. Negative thoughts will lead to negative feelings and behaviors. Therefore, CBT attempts to change a person's pattern of negative thinking and behaviors. IPT focuses on a patient's relationships with others, at work and at home. The therapist helps the patient understand how interacting with other people affects the patient's moods. Psychodynamic therapy focuses on how life events and relationships affect the patient's feelings and choices. Together, a patient and therapist work to identify and understand how past events influence the patient's present behavior.

## Antidepressants

Medication is often prescribed for managing moderate to severe depression. According to a 2011 Harvard Medical School Special Health Report on depression, antidepressants can give 65 to 85 percent of patients some relief from depression symptoms. Antidepressant medications work by adjusting mood-related brain chemicals such as serotonin and norepinephrine to normal levels. There are several types of antidepressants, including selective serotonin reuptake inhibitors (SSRIs), tricyclics, and monoamine oxidase inhibitors (MAOIs).

Antidepressants are not without drawbacks, however. Many have serious side effects. These include nausea, weight gain or loss, anxiety, insomnia, dry mouth, dizziness, and fatigue. They may also cause agitation, restlessness, tics, and tremors. Some may cause a serious disturbance of a patient's heart rhythms, while others can cause high blood pressure and abnormal liver function. Some patients stop taking their medication because of the side effects—a decision that often leads to a recurrence of depression. According to the National Alliance on Mental Illness, an estimated 50 percent of unsuccessful depression treatment is due to people's not taking their medicine or not taking it correctly.

> " Up to 80 percent of patients see an improvement in their symptoms within four to six weeks of beginning treatment. "

Of growing concern in recent years are reports of links between antidepressants and suicide, especially in adolescents. "The FDA [U.S. Food and Drug Administration] has warned that children and adults may show suicidal behavior in the first weeks of treatment with these drugs, but the actual role is not clear," says Penny B. Donnenfeld, a psychologist in New York City. "There have been cases where suicide was linked to antidepressants, but whether that was the nature of the depression, a slight relief from depressive symptoms, or an actual effect of a drug side effect causing increased agitation and anxiety is not clear."[48]

## Overprescribing of Antidepressants

Additionally, antidepressants may not work for every patient. A 2010 analysis from researchers at the University of Pennsylvania concluded that antidepressants work best for patients with the most severe symptoms. For those with mild to moderate depression, the benefits were less noticeable. "There is little evidence to suggest that [antidepressants] produce specific pharmacological benefit for the majority of patients with less severe acute depression,"[49] the study's researchers concluded.

Despite this research, the overprescribing of antidepressants—specifically for patients who do not meet the criteria for clinical depression—is a concern. According to a 2011 Centers for Disease Control and Prevention report, antidepressant use increased more than 400 percent over a ten-year period ending in 2008. Mental health expert Gordon Parker, a professor at the University of South Wales in Australia, says that doctors often diagnose patients with depression too quickly and that depression has become a catch-all label for normal emotional states. Patients with normal low moods are being prescribed antidepressant medication even though research shows that it is less effective for such patients.

## Other Treatments

In addition to talk therapy and medication, other treatments are available for depression. Five to 10 percent of major depression episodes require hospitalization. This occurs most often when patients have become a threat to themselves or others. In most cases, this involves involuntary commitment of the patient initiated by a relative or friend. In the hospital, doctors and nurses can provide more intensive therapy and closer monitoring than would be available outside the hospital setting.

For severe cases of depression that do not respond well to medication and talk therapy, electroconvulsive therapy (ECT) may be used. ECT is especially effective for those who are extremely depressed or suicidal. According to Harvard Medical School, 80 to 90 percent of depressed patients initially respond to ECT treatment. During ECT, electrodes deliver electrical impulses to locations on the head. While the patient does not feel the impulses, the electrical stimulation causes a thirty-second seizure in the brain. Doctors believe ECT affects the chemical balance of the

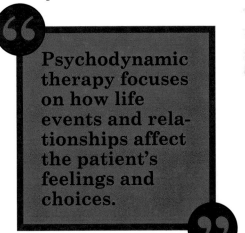

Psychodynamic therapy focuses on how life events and relationships affect the patient's feelings and choices.

brain's neurotransmitters. "People whose lives have been affected by severe treatment-resistant depression deserve the best that medical science has to offer, and today that is ECT,"[50] says Sarah Lisanby, chair of the Department of Psychiatry at Duke University.

Julie Hersh, a patient with major depression, felt the effects of ECT after the first treatment. She recalls, "Even after just one treatment I was better. I'd finally surfaced on the other side of a wave that had swallowed me for nine months. My depression had trapped me in a watery cage. . . . Finally, I burst through the water . . . [and] in an instant, I could breathe again."[51]

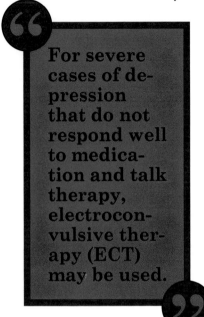

For severe cases of depression that do not respond well to medication and talk therapy, electroconvulsive therapy (ECT) may be used.

ECT is not without risks. Short-term memory loss is one of the most common side effects. While some memory function may return after treatment ends, problems may remain. Some patients report that they use daily planners and lists to help with memory after ECT. Another drawback to ECT is that approximately 50 percent of patients with severe depression relapse after initial treatment, according to the Harvard Medical School. To prevent relapse, some people take antidepressants or receive monthly maintenance ECT treatments after their initial treatment.

For people with seasonal affective disorder (SAD), light therapy is an effective treatment. Patients spend about half an hour per day in front of a specially designed light box that mimics outdoor light. Doctors believe that the intense light causes a biochemical change in the brain that lifts mood and reduces SAD symptoms.

## Stimulating Nerves

When other depression treatments do not work, some patients receive transcranial magnetic stimulation (TMS), which is designed to stimulate nerves in the brain. During TMS, a special electromagnet is placed on the patient's scalp and generates short magnetic pulses. The pulses pass through the skull, stimulating the brain. Research has shown that TMS alters brain chemistry in such a way that it is as effective as medication at relieving depression symptoms, but without the side effects of medication. TMS may have long-term benefits as well. Research presented at the 2010 American Psychiatric Association meeting found that only about 10 to 12 percent of patients who achieve remission using TMS relapsed in the six months following therapy.

Vagus nerve stimulation (VNS) can be used to alleviate treatment-resistant depression in adults. The vagus nerve is found on each side of the body, running from the brainstem through the neck and down the chest and abdomen. VNS therapy surgically implants a small pulse generator in the patient's chest and connects it to the vagus nerve. The generator sends small pulses to the vagus nerve, which in turn delivers the pulses to the brain. VNS therapy targets the areas of the brain that control depression symptoms and mood. Common side effects with VNS include hoarseness, cough, and neck pain, although these may subside over time.

## Lifestyle Changes

While it is not always possible to prevent depression, certain lifestyle changes can reduce the risk and severity of depression. According to the American Psychiatric Association, a healthy lifestyle is an important factor in the brain's ability to regulate mood. Eating well, exercising, and getting enough sleep are all good ways to keep the body in balance. Exercise also releases chemicals called endorphins into the brain, a natural way to lift mood and boost energy.

Managing stress is another way to reduce vulnerability to depression. "Excessive stress impairs your ability to find solutions, to keep on making productive choices, and to mobilize the energy to continue going forward. For many people, excessive stress is the trigger for depression,"[52] says psychologist Margaret Wehrenberg. Some people use art and writing as a way to release stress. Others focus on simplifying and cutting back on unnecessary activities, staying positive, and learning to recognize the warning signs of stress.

> According to the American Psychiatric Association, a healthy lifestyle is an important factor in the brain's ability to regulate mood.

Another key to managing depression is getting support. "If you are depressed, one of the best ways to break out of isolation is to get some social support right away,"[53] says Wehrenberg. Support may come from family, friends, a therapist, or a support group of people who have experienced depression. Many people find that joining a support group and meeting others with similar experiences helps them manage their disorder. While support groups and lifestyle changes are not a cure for depression, they can reduce the factors that contribute to the illness.

## Unsuccessful Treatment

Antidepressants offer help to many—but not all—people who suffer from depression. According to the American Academy of Family Physicians, between one-third and two-thirds of patients will not respond to the first antidepressant prescribed. Fifteen to 33 percent will not respond after multiple medications or combinations of medications. These patients may suffer from treatment-resistant depression. In these cases, doctors may try alternative medications and treatments.

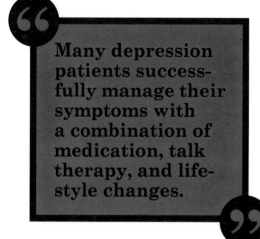

**Many depression patients successfully manage their symptoms with a combination of medication, talk therapy, and lifestyle changes.**

In some cases, people with depression do not seek treatment. According to a 2010 study published in the *Archives of General Psychiatry,* only half of all people with depression received treatment. Moreover, among those who did receive treatment, only 21 percent received treatment that was consistent with American Psychiatric Association guidelines.

Nontreatment and undertreatment of depression is a result of many factors, including the lack of health insurance, financial barriers, and ignorance about treatment benefits. One of the greatest barriers to treatment is the stigma of having a mental illness. Many people may be afraid to tell others about their symptoms and to ask for help.

## Finding Hope from Treatment

Many depression patients successfully manage their symptoms with a combination of medication, talk therapy, and lifestyle changes. They gather a strong support system that can help during difficult times, and they educate themselves about their illness. In addition, new treatments and research bring hope for treating depression in the future.

Because depression affects each person differently, it may take time for any given patient to find the right combination of treatments to ease symptoms. Beth-Sarah Wright says that every day is another step in her journey of living with depression. With medication and talk therapy, she is working to regain her health. "I have not reached the point where I would say everything is just right," she says. "But I'm working on it every day. Every day. I've had to learn how to re-love my children, re-love my husband, re-love myself. It's a process, and . . . it takes patience. It doesn't happen overnight."[54]

# What Treatments Are Available for Depressive Disorders?

**66** The science of psychiatric pharmaceuticals has improved dramatically in the past 15 years. My psychiatrist has worked up for me a cocktail of mood levelers to treat my manic-depression. **99**

—Tim McGhee, "Sports and Mental Illness: How Bipolar Disorder Can Affect Athletic Performance," Bleacher Report, December 28, 2010. http://bleacherreport.com.

McGhee is a correspondent for the sports website Bleacher Report and suffers from bipolar disorder.

**66** Antidepressants do have a function in relieving a person's symptoms, influencing chemical messengers in the brain to lift a person's mood. But I do question their use on mild depression as the side effects often outweigh the benefits. **99**

—Funke Baffour, "It's Good to Talk—Therapy Not Pills for Depression," BBC News, October 15, 2010. www.bbc.co.uk.

Baffour is a clinical psychologist in the United Kingdom.

* Editor's Note: While the definition of a primary source can be narrowly or broadly defined, for the purposes of Compact Research, a primary source consists of: 1) results of original research presented by an organization or researcher; 2) eyewitness accounts of events, personal experience, or work experience; 3) first-person editorials offering pundits' opinions; 4) government officials presenting political plans and/or policies; 5) representatives of organizations presenting testimony or policy.

> **❝ECT works even when psychotherapy or medications fail, and studies report that up to 80 to 90 percent of people experience a complete recovery. ECT is an indispensable part of mainstream medicine.❞**

—Sarah Lisanby, presentation to the U.S. Food and Drug Administration Neurological Devices Panel, January 27, 2011. http://psychcentral.com.

Lisanby chairs the Department of Psychiatry at Duke University and the American Psychiatric Association Task Force on ECT.

---

> **❝But the just-get-people-into-treatment message misses something more fundamental. Our supposedly effective treatments for depression are not all that effective.❞**

—Jonathan Rottenberg, "We Need Better Depression Treatment, Not Simply More," *Psychology Today*, January 5, 2010.

Rottenberg is associate professor of psychology at the University of South Florida and the director of the universitiy's Mood and Emotion Laboratory.

---

> **❝Depression isn't a prerequisite for introspection, but it did lead me to the psychotherapy that has given me a greater understanding of myself.❞**

—Bruce Clark, "Fighting for Self-Awareness," *Esperanza*, Fall 2010.

Clark is a writer and stand-up comedian who was diagnosed with depression in his early thirties.

---

> **❝Getting better from depression demands a lifelong commitment.❞**

—Susan Polis Schutz, "Hearing Echoes of Optimism," *Esperanza*, Fall 2010.

Schutz is cofounder of Blue Mountain Arts publishing and a depression patient.

---

**❝Finding a therapist you click with can be as hard as finding a soulmate. Not every counselor is a good fit— and even a good fit won't always stay that way.❞**

—Jenny Stamos, "Trying on Therapists," *Esperanza*, Summer 2011.

Stamos has dysthymia.

---

**❝For me, staying on medication is an essential element that keeps my depression from coming back full-throttle.❞**

—Deborah Serani, "Preventing Relapse," *Esperanza*, Summer 2011.

Serani is a psychologist specializing in treating depression and trauma who also suffers from depression herself.

---

**❝I began to work with cognitive behavioral therapy (CBT) techniques and learned that dysfunctional thinking patterns could be contributing to my low moods.❞**

—Vincent Caimano, "In Charge of Change," *Esperanza*, Summer 2011.

Caimano is the founder of Depression Recovery Groups and is himself a depression patient.

---

# What Treatments Are Available for Depressive Disorders?

- Only about **half** of Americans diagnosed with major depression in a given year receive treatment for the illness, according to the National Alliance for Mental Illness (NAMI).

- According to the CDC, about one in ten people in the United States aged twelve and over are taking **antidepressant medication**.

- The CDC says that more than **60 percent** of Americans who take antidepressant medication have taken it for two years or longer, with 14 percent having taken the medication for ten years or more.

- About **50 percent** of unsuccessful treatments for depression results from people not following their doctor's instructions, reports the Depression and Bipolar Support Alliance.

- Support group participants are **86 percent** more willing to take medication and to cope with side effects, according to the Depression and Bipolar Support Alliance.

- Up to 10 percent of major depressive episodes and **50 percent** of manic episodes require hospitalization.

## Depression Treatments

A variety of standard and alternative treatments are available for people with depression—and some have shown better results than others. According to a *Consumer Reports* poll of its online subscribers, prescription medication is the most widely used and effective treatment for depression. Other treatments such as meditation, yoga, massage, and deep-breathing exercises were also cited as helping people with depression.

| Depression Treatments | % Who Used | % Helped a Lot |
|---|---|---|
| Prescription medication | 80% | 69% |
| Meditation | 21% | 36% |
| Yoga | 10% | 35% |
| Deep-tissue massage | 10% | 28% |
| Deep-breathing exercises | 18% | 22% |
| Over-the-counter medication | 7% | 15% |
| Vitamin B complex | 14% | 13% |
| Fish-oil supplements | 15% | 10% |
| Multivitamins | 18% | 8% |

Source: *Consumer Reports*, "Depression," September 2011. www.consumerreports.org.

- **Cognitive behavioral therapy** is not a traditional, long-term talk therapy; it usually lasts for only ten to twenty weeks, says NAMI.

## Prevalence of Antidepressant Medication

According to the Centers for Disease Control and Prevention, about one in ten Americans over age twelve takes antidepressant medication. In fact, the CDC reports that antidepressants are the third most common prescription medication taken by all Americans. Females were more likely to take anti-depressants than males, at every age group. The majority of people who use antidepressants use them to treat depression, although some anti-depressants are used for treating other disorders.

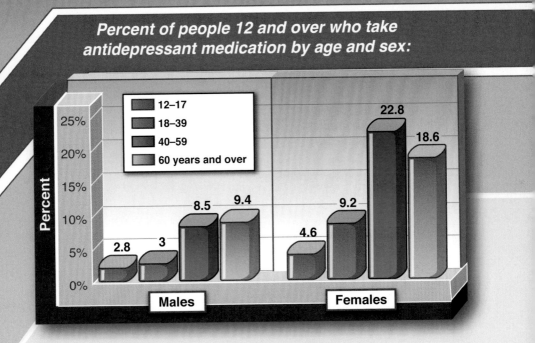

**Percent of people 12 and over who take antidepressant medication by age and sex:**

Source: Centers for Disease Control and Prevention, "Antidepressant Use in Persons Aged 12 and Over, United States: 2005–2008," NCHS Data Brief, no. 34, October 2011. www.cdc.gov.

- A study from the University of Texas Southwest Medical Center reports that thirty minutes of **aerobic exercise** three to five times per week reduced depression symptoms in almost **50 percent** of participants.

# Barriers to Treatment

Mental health experts say that early and appropriate treatment is key to recovery from depression. However, many people who suffer from mental illness, including depression, do not seek treatment. Cost of mental health care services is the primary barrier to seeking treatment, according to research published in 2012 by the American Hospital Association. Patients also cite the belief that they can take care of the problem without treatment, lack of time, and not having health insurance coverage.

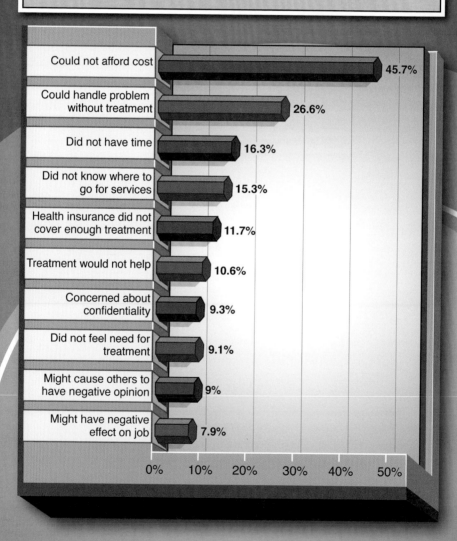

| Barrier | Percentage |
|---|---|
| Could not afford cost | 45.7% |
| Could handle problem without treatment | 26.6% |
| Did not have time | 16.3% |
| Did not know where to go for services | 15.3% |
| Health insurance did not cover enough treatment | 11.7% |
| Treatment would not help | 10.6% |
| Concerned about confidentiality | 9.3% |
| Did not feel need for treatment | 9.1% |
| Might cause others to have negative opinion | 9% |
| Might have negative effect on job | 7.9% |

Source: American Hospital Association, "Trendwatch: Bringing Behavioral Health into the Care Continuum: Opportunities to Improve Quality, Costs and Outcomes," January 2012. www.aha.org.

- Only **21 percent** of Americans with major depression receive minimally adequate care, according to a study published in the January 2010 *Archives in General Psychiatry*.

- If two to three drug treatments fail, a person may be considered **treatment resistant**, according to Families for Depression Awareness.

- According to the Cleveland Clinic, patients with seasonal affective disorder who receive **light therapy** have shown some improvement within two to four days and reach full benefits within two to four weeks.

- Antidepressants may take **two to four weeks** to start taking effect and need **six to twelve weeks** to have their full effect, according to NAMI.

# Key People and Advocacy Groups

**American Psychiatric Association:** Publisher of the *Diagnostic and Statistical Manual of Mental Disorders*, the American Psychiatric Association guides the country's thirty-eight thousand psychiatrists on treating mental illnesses, including depression. The association's advocacy efforts include educating the public about mental health, psychiatry, and successful treatment options.

**The Balanced Mind Foundation:** A not-for-profit organization of families who are raising children and teens affected by depression, bipolar disorder, and other mood disorders.

**Depression and Bipolar Support Alliance:** The leading patient-directed national organization focusing on depression and bipolar disorder, the alliance supports research to promote more timely diagnoses, develop more effective treatments, and discover a cure for depressive disorders.

**Zack Greinke:** Major League Baseball pitcher who missed most of the 2006 season while being treated for depression. His case is considered groundbreaking in helping major league players remove the stigma attached to mental health issues.

**Demi Lovato:** A well-known young actress and singer who has revealed that she has been diagnosed with bipolar disorder, bringing the issue to the attention of adolescents across the country.

**Mental Health America:** The country's largest and oldest community-based network consists of more than three hundred affiliates dedicated to helping all people live mentally healthier lives. The organization advocates for policy change, educates the public, and provides community programs and services.

**National Alliance on Mental Illness (NAMI):** A grassroots mental health advocacy organization that works to increase awareness, provide education, and advocate for policy change that improves the lives of people with mental illnesses, including depression.

**National Institute of Mental Health (NIMH):** A part of the National Institutes of Health and one of the world's leading mental health organizations, NIMH conducts and supports research on the causes, diagnosis, prevention, and treatment of depression and other mood disorders.

**Brooke Shields:** A well-known actress who wrote about her experience with postpartum depression in her book *Down Came the Rain*. She has also spoken out about removing the social stigma of postpartum depression.

**Mike Wallace:** An editor at the top-rated *60 Minutes* television newsmagazine, Wallace developed depression during a long court trial where his integrity and judgment were questioned daily. Years after seeking treatment, Wallace spoke out on television about his experience with depression, hoping to inspire people to seek help.

# Chronology

**1937**
Italian researchers Ugo Cerletti and Lucio Bini introduce electrically induced seizures to treat mental illness, the only form of electroconvulsive therapy accepted today.

**1917**
Sigmund Freud writes about melancholia, or extreme depression, and emphasizes that early life experiences may contribute to this condition.

**1957**
Iproniazid, one of the first antidepressants, is synthesized. Originally developed as a treatment for tuberculosis, it was widely prescribed in the late 1950s to treat depression.

1910

1935

1960

**1949**
The National Institute of Mental Health is formally established on April 15.

**1924**
American psychologist Mary Cover Jones introduces a therapeutic behavioral approach to helping children unlearn fears. Behavioral therapy would eventually be merged with cognitive therapy to form cognitive behavioral therapy.

**1952**
The American Psychiatric Association publishes the first *Diagnostic and Statistical Manual of Mental Disorders* (DSM), which is widely used today by clinicians and researchers in the United States and around the world to diagnose and treat mental disorders, including depressive disorders.

**1975**
The National Institute of Mental Health Conference on Depression in Childhood officially recognizes depression in children.

**2011**
Researchers find a section of chromosome 3 that is associated with depression.

**1985**
The Depression and Bipolar Support Alliance is founded in Chicago and becomes one of the largest national organizations to provide support to people with depression.

**2009**
Researchers using brain imaging find that people with a thinning of the brain's right cortex have a higher risk of developing depression.

**1975**

**2000**

**2005**
The U.S. Food and Drug Administration approves the use of vagus nerve stimulation to treat treatment-resistant depression.

**1988**
The first selective serotonin reuptake inhibitor (SSRI) antidepressant, known as Prozac, launches in the United States, becoming one of the biggest-selling drugs in history.

**2008**
President George W. Bush signs the Mental Health Parity and Addiction Equity Act, which requires health insurers to provide coverage for mental illnesses, including depression, equal to the coverage provided for physical illnesses.

**1979**
The National Alliance on Mental Illness (NAMI) is founded to provide support, education, advocacy, and research services for people with serious psychiatric illnesses.

**2012**
UCLA researchers find that people with depression appear to have hyperactive brains.

# Related Organizations

### American Academy of Child and Adolescent Psychiatry (AACAP)

3615 Wisconsin Ave. NW
Washington, DC 20016
phone: (202) 966-7300 • fax: (202) 966-2891
website: www.aacap.org

The academy is a national professional medical association dedicated to treating and improving the quality of life for children, adolescents, and families affected by mental, behavioral, or developmental disorders. Its website offers fact sheets and provides the locations of resource centers with information on depression, bipolar disorder, and other mental illnesses.

### American Foundation for Suicide Prevention (AFSP)

120 Wall St., 29th Floor
New York, NY 10005
toll-free phone: (888) 333-2377 • fax: (212) 363-6237
e-mail: inquiry@afsp.org • website: www.afsp.org

The AFSP is the leading national not-for-profit organization dedicated to understanding and preventing suicide through research, education, and advocacy. Its website provides information and fact sheets on depression and bipolar disorder.

### American Psychiatric Association

1000 Wilson Blvd., Suite 1825
Arlington, VA 22209-3901
toll-free phone: (888) 357-7924
e-mail: apa@psych.org • website: www.psych.org

The American Psychiatric Association has more than thirty-eight thousand US and international member physicians working together to ensure humane care and effective treatment for all persons with mental disorders. The association publishes many books and journals, including the widely read *American Journal of Psychiatry*.

Related Organizations

## American Psychological Association

750 First St. NE
Washington, DC 20002-4242
toll-free phone: (800) 374-2721
e-mail: public.affairs@apa.org • website: www.apa.org

The American Psychological Association represents more than 148,000 professional American psychologists who study and treat human behavior. Its website features information about psychology topics, including depression and links to many publications.

## Association for Behavioral and Cognitive Therapies (ABCT)

305 Seventh Ave., 16th Floor
New York, NY 10001
phone: (212) 647-1890 • fax: (212) 647-1865
website: www.abct.org

This association represents therapists who provide cognitive behavioral therapy for people who suffer from many types of mental illnesses, including depression. Its website features fact sheets on mental illnesses, including depression and bipolar disorders.

## The Balanced Mind Foundation

566 W. Lake St., Suite 430
Chicago, IL 60661
phone: (847) 492-8510
e-mail: info@thebalancedmind.org
website: www.thebalancedmind.org

The Balanced Mind Foundation is a not-for-profit organization of families with children and teens affected by depression, bipolar disorder, and other mood disorders. The group's website has information about depression, bipolar disorder, and current research.

## Depression and Bipolar Support Alliance (DBSA)

730 N. Franklin St., Suite 501
Chicago, IL 60654-7225
toll-free phone: (800) 826-3632 • fax: (312) 642-7243
e-mail: info@dbsalliance.org • website: www.dbsalliance.org

The Depression and Bipolar Support Alliance has more than four hundred community-based chapters that provide support for people with depressive disorders and their families. Its website provides a variety of information about depression, treatments, and research.

## Families for Depression Awareness

395 Totten Pond Rd., Suite 404
Waltham, MA 02451
phone: (781) 890-0220
website: www.familyaware.org

Families for Depression Awareness is a nonprofit organization that helps people and their families recognize and cope with depression and bipolar disorders. The group's website features information about depression and symptoms, support groups, and family profiles.

## Mental Health America (MHA)

2000 N. Beauregard St., 6th Floor
Alexandria, VA 22311
toll-free phone: (800) 969-6642 • fax: (703) 684-5968
email: info@mentalhealthamerica.net • website: www.nmha.org

Mental Health America is an advocacy group for people with mental illnesses and their families. Its website features many resources, including fact sheets on mood disorders, listings of support groups, and suggestions for how to take action to support research and funding for the treatment of mental illnesses.

## National Alliance on Mental Illness (NAMI)

3803 N. Fairfax Dr., Suite 100
Arlington, VA 22203
phone: (703) 524-7600 • fax: (703) 524-9094
website: www.nami.org

The NAMI is an advocacy group for people with mental illnesses and includes local chapters in every state. It offers education programs and services for individuals and family members. Its website has news and information about depression research, treatment, support groups, and more.

## National Institute of Mental Health (NIMH)

6001 Executive Blvd., Room 8184, MSC 9663
Bethesda, MD 20892-9663
toll-free phone: (866) 615-6464 • fax: (301) 443-4279
e-mail: nimhinfo@nih.gov • website: www.nimh.nih.gov

The National Institute of Mental Health is the federal government's chief funding agency for mental health research in America. Its website provides fact sheets and information about mental illnesses, including depression, and the latest science news and research on these illnesses.

# For Further Research

## Books

Rachel Eagen, *Suicide*. New York: Crabtree, 2011.

Roman Espejo, *Mental Illness: Opposing Viewpoints*. Detroit: Greenhaven, 2011.

Harvard Health Publications, "Understanding Depression," Special Health Report, 2011.

Julie K. Hersh, *Struck by Living: From Depression to Hope*. Austin, TX: Greenleaf, 2011.

Abigail Meisel, *Investigating Depression and Bipolar Disorder: Real Facts for Real Lives*. Berkeley Heights, NJ: Enslow, 2011.

Carla Mooney, *Mental Illness Research*. San Diego: ReferencePoint, 2012.

Wendy Moragne, *Depression*. Minneapolis: Twenty-First Century, 2011.

Michael L. Owens and Amy Gelman, *I'm Depressed, Now What?* New York: Rosen, 2012.

## Periodicals

Janice Arenofsky, "The Stigma Within," *Esperanza*, Winter 2011.

Clive Cookson, "Scientists Find Genetic Link to Depression," *Financial Times*, May 16, 2011.

Karen Crouse, "For Renewed Wright, Sport Is a Game Again," *New York Times*, March 29, 2012.

Jennifer Corbett Dooren, "Effectiveness of Antidepressants Varies Widely," *Wall Street Journal*, January 6, 2010.

*Glamour*, "Interview: I Thought If I Disappeared It Wouldn't Matter," May 17, 2012.

Jodi Helmer, "Physical Signs of Depression: Hear Your Body Talk!," *Esperanza*, Fall 2010.

Jodi Helmer, "Worth Fighting For," *Esperanza*, Summer 2012.

Sharon Jayson, "Brain 'Hyperconnectivity' Linked to Depression," *USA Today*, February 21, 2012.

Scott Pitoniak, "Everyday Heroes: The Professor's Education," *Esperanza*, Summer 2011.

Roni Caryn Rabin, "A Portable Glow to Help Melt Those Winter Blues," *New York Times*, November 14, 2011.

## Internet Sources

CBS News, "Depression Blood Test for Teens May Lead to Better Treatment, Less Stigma," April 17, 2012. www.cbsnews.com/8301-504 763_162-57415188-10391704/depression-blood-test-for-teens -may-lead-to-better-treatment-less-stigma.

Kat Kinsman, "Going Public with Depression," CNN, August 22, 2012. www.cnn.com/2012/08/22/living/going-public-with-depression /index.html.

# Source Notes

## Overview

1. Quoted in Karen Crouse, "For Renewed Wright, Sport Is a Game Again," *New York Times*, March 29, 2012. www.nytimes.com.
2. Harvard Health Publications, "Understanding Depression," Special Health Report, 2011, p. 5.
3. Quoted in Clive Cookson, "Scientists Find Genetic Link to Depression," *Financial Times*, May 16, 2011. www.ft.com.
4. Quoted in National Alliance on Mental Illness, "Depression," 2012, p. 5. www.nami.org.
5. Quoted in Janice Arenofsky, "The Stigma Within," *Esperanza*, Winter 2011. www.hopetocope.com.
6. Quoted in Jodi Helmer, "Worth Fighting For . . . ," *Esperanza*, Summer 2012. www.hopetocope.com.
7. Quoted in Dennis Thompson Jr., "Depression and Substance Abuse," Everyday Health, June 30, 2011. www.everydayhealth.com.
8. Students Against Depression, "Real Student Stories: Pete," 2011–2012. www.studentdepression.org.
9. Quoted in Families for Depression Awareness, "Ashley, Age 19, with Clinical Depression and Anxiety . . . ," www.familyaware.org.
10. Quoted in CBS News, "Depression Blood Test for Teens May Lead to Better Treatment, Less Stigma," April 17, 2012. www.cbsnews.com.
11. Quoted in National Alliance on Mental Illness, "Depression," p. 6.
12. Quoted in Arenofsky, "The Stigma Within."
13. Quoted in Arenofsky, "The Stigma Within."
14. Quoted in Arenofsky, "The Stigma Within."

## What Are Depressive Disorders?

15. Quoted in "Depression Survivors Describe What It Really Feels Like," *Health*, April 11, 2008. www.health.com.
16. Quoted in *Esperanza*, "Sound Off! Physical Signs of Depression," Fall 2010, p. 31.
17. Quoted in Roni Caryn Rabin, "A Portable Glow to Help Melt Those Winter Blues," *New York Times*, November 14, 2011. www.nytimes.com.
18. Quoted in Rabin, "A Portable Glow to Help Melt Those Winter Blues."
19. Quoted in *US News & World Report, Alpha Consumer* (blog), "Postpartum Depression: Finding Affordable Help," June 14, 2011. http://money.usnews.com.
20. Laura Schiller, "Postpartum Depression," Goop, July 2010. http://goop.com.
21. Quoted in *Us Weekly*, "Bipolar Demi Lovato Talks Cutting, Eating Disorders," April 21, 2011. www.usmagazine.com.
22. Quoted in *Glamour*, "Interview: I Thought If I Disappeared It Wouldn't Matter," May 17, 2012. www.glamourmagazine.co.uk.
23. Quoted in *Glamour*, "Interview."
24. Quoted in *Glamour*, "Interview."

## What Causes Depressive Disorders?

25. Harvard Health Publications, "Understanding Depression," p. 5.
26. Quoted in Nick Collins, "Women More than Twice as Likely to Be Depressed," *Daily Telegraph* (London), September 5, 2011. www.telegraph.co.uk.
27. Quoted in *ScienceDaily*, "Resurrecting the So-Called 'Depression Gene': New Evidence That Our Genes Play a Role in Our Response to Adversity," January 4, 2011. www.sciencedaily.com.
28. Quoted in Cookson, "Scientists Find Genetic Link to Depression."

29. Quoted in Courtney Hutchison, "Gene Variant Could Predict Chance of Depression," ABC News, January 4, 2011. http://abcnews.go.com.

30. Quoted in Margarita Tartakovsky, "A Current Look at Chronic Depression," PsychCentral, 2012. http://psychcentral.com.

31. Quoted in Sharon Jayson, "Brain 'Hyperconnectivity' Linked to Depression," *USA Today*, February 21, 2012. www.usatoday.com.

32. Quoted in Mark Wheeler, "Hyperactivity in Brain May Explain Multiple Symptoms of Depression," UCLA Newsroom, February 27, 2012. http://newsroom.ucla.edu.

33. Students Against Depression, "Real Student Stories: Donna," 2011–2012. www.studentdepression.org.

34. Quoted in *ScienceDaily*, "Childhood Maltreatment Linked to Long-Term Depression Risk and Poor Response to Treatment," August 13, 2011. www.sciencedaily.com.

## How Do Depressive Disorders Affect People?

35. Kat Kinsman, "Going Public with Depression," CNN, August 22, 2012. www.cnn.com.

36. Quoted in Jodi Helmer, "Physical Signs of Depression: Hear Your Body Talk!," *Esperanza*, Fall 2010. www.hopetocope.com.

37. Quoted in Helmer, "Physical Signs of Depression."

38. Quoted in Scott Pitoniak, "Everyday Heroes: The Professor's Education," *Esperanza*, Summer 2011, p.28.

39. Students Against Depression, "Real Student Stories: Safa," 2008–2009. www.studentdepression.org.

40. Students Against Depression, "Real Student Stories: Lauren," 2011–2012. www.studentdepression.org.

41. Quoted in Wyatt Myers, "Depression: How to Challenge Negative Thinking," Everyday Health, August 6, 2012. www.everydayhealth.com.

42. Quoted in Myers," Depression."

43. Quoted in Pitoniak, "Everyday Heroes, p. 28.

44. Quoted in Jodi Helmer, "The Ripple Effect," *Esperanza*, Spring 2011. www.hopetocope.com.

45. Quoted in Helmer, "The Ripple Effect."

46. Quoted in Mikaela Conley, "Mike Wallace's Battle with Depression and Suicide," ABC News, April 9, 2012. http://abcnews.go.com.

## What Treatments Are Available for Depressive Disorders?

47. American Psychological Association, "Understanding Depression and Effective Treatment." www.apa.org.

48. Quoted in Wyatt Myers, "Depression, Antidepressants, and Suicide Risk," EverydayHealth, May 3, 2010. www.everydayhealth.com.

49. Quoted in Jennifer Corbett Dooren, "Effectiveness of Antidepressants Varies Widely," *Wall Street Journal*, January 6, 2010. www.wsj.com.

50. Sarah Lisanby, presentation to the U.S. Food and Drug Administration Neurological Devices Panel, January 27, 2011. http://psychcentral.com.

51. Julie Hersh, *Struck by Living: From Depression to Hope*. Austin, TX: Greenleaf, 2011, p.28.

52. Margaret Wehrenberg, *The 10 Best-Ever Depression Management Techniques*. New York: Norton, 2010. p. 121.

53. Wehrenberg, *The 10 Best-Ever Depression Management Techniques*, p. 145.

54. Quoted in Pitoniak, "Everyday Heroes," p. 29.

# List of Illustrations

List of Illustrations

# Index

aches and pains, 49–50
adolescents
    antidepressant use by, 75 (graph)
    and cognitive effects of depression, 50–51
    and onset of bipolar disorder, 27
    and risk factors for depression, 36, 43
    prevalence of depression in, 11, 32, 34
      (graph)
    substance abuse by, 52, 59
    suicide and, 58, 64
    and undermining of developmental skills,
      56
adults, prevalence of depression in, 8, 11, 34
    (graph)
alcohol abuse, 16, 17 (illustration)
    *See also* substance abuse
All About Depression, 34, 45
alternative treatments, 74 (chart)
American Academy of Child & Adolescent
    Psychiatry, 45
American Foundation for Suicide Prevention,
    53
American Hospital Association, 76
*American Journal of Psychiatry,* 41
American Psychiatric Association, 67, 68
American Psychological Association, 63
anorexia, 24
antidepressant medications
    action on brain chemicals by, 19, 63–64
    and criteria for treatment resistant
      diagnosis, 77
    ECT combined with, 66
    effectiveness of, 19–20, 63, 68, 74 (chart)
    improvements in, 70
    overprescribing of, 64–65
    types of, 19, 65
    use of
      by age and gender, 75 (graph)
      duration for, 73, 77
      improper, 19–20
      side effects and, 64, 70
      by support group participants, 73
anxiety disorders, 58

appetite. *See* eating patterns
*Archives in General Psychiatry* (journal), 77

baby blues. *See* postpartum depression
Bach, Rick, 26
Baffour, Funke, 70
behavioral effects, 16, 52
    *See also* substance abuse
Bennett, Chuck, 22
bipolar disorder
    age at onset of, 27
    described, 27, 30
    hospitalization for, 73
    prevalence of, 11, 33 (graph)
      genetic risk factor and, 36–37, 45
    workdays lost to, 58
blood test, 19
brain
    chemistry of
      action by antidepressants on, 19, 63–64
      ECT and, 65
      endorphins, 67
      imbalances in, as cause, 13, 39
      TMS and, 66
    hormones and, 13–14, 47
    structure and function of, 38–39, 47
      (illustration)
Breen, Gerome, 37
bulimia, 24
businesses, cost to, 15

Caimano, Vincent, 43, 72
cancer, 24, 45, 61
Carlton, Catherine, 26
causes. *See* risk factors
Centers for Disease Control and Prevention
    (CDC)
    on annual suicide rate, 16
    on overprescribing of antidepressants, 65
    on prevalence of depression in adults, 11,
      32
    on suicide attempts, 53–54
    on suicide incidence, 53

# About the Author

Carla Mooney is the author of many books for young adults and children. She lives in Pittsburgh, Pennsylvania, with her husband and three children.